THE ROCKET MODEL

PRACTICAL ADVICE FOR BUILDING HIGH PERFORMING TEAMS

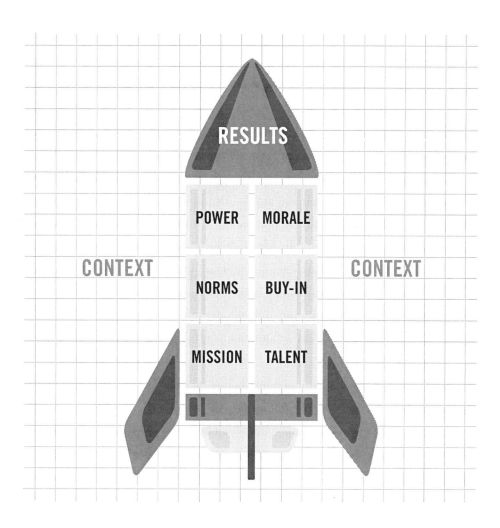

RESULTS

POWER   MORALE

CONTEXT   NORMS   BUY-IN   CONTEXT

MISSION   TALENT

GORDON CURPHY | ROBERT HOGAN

The Rocket Model
Practical Advice for Building High Performing Teams

By Gordon Curphy and Robert Hogan

Hogan Press
2622 E 21st Street Tulsa, OK 74114
www.hoganpress.com

ISBN 978-0-9840969-8-5

ISBN: 978-0-9840969-8-5

9 780984 096985

"This book rocks! The Rocket Model is an easy to use diagnostic and team improvement framework that leaders at all levels can embrace and use every day. The practical application is immediate, profound and long lasting. It fosters continuous improvement and equips leaders to assess their teams, improve team dynamics and then replicate the process again and again. At Waste Management, we trained over 1,000 District Managers on how to use this model and saw immediate improvements in team effectiveness and employee engagement. This is a tool you don't want to miss out on!"

> – Jimmy LaValley
> Senior Vice President and Chief People Officer,
> Waste Management, Inc., (Retired)

"Driving "successful" transformational change through employee commitment and buy-in is crucial. Those leaders that transform their groups into transparent, collaborative and engaged teams will be successful and beat their competition.

The Rocket Model was instrumental in allowing us to build key foundations in core areas required to support the successful transformation of our company into a global matrix. We will continue to use this great tool as change is constant and the need to build high performing teams is critical for future success."

> – Paul Keane
> Executive Vice President, Human Resources
> CSA Group

"This book should be requisite reading for anyone who aspires to a leadership role in business, academics, government, civic service – or life in general. Importantly, it also speaks to those who just strive to be better employees, members, and citizens.

Gordon Curphy and Bob Hogan re-define successful leadership and teamwork today. More important, they anticipate what both will require in the future. Their use of actual business and sports examples to illustrate group dynamics, distinguish the true elements of effective teamwork, and separate out the critical elements of progressive leadership is outstanding.

This book shouldn't stay on the shelf but, rather, be a daily companion guide that reminds, instructs, and informs us all at every turn. Gordon and Bob map a culture of personal and professional engagement that can become a critical tool for success in business and life. I hope it becomes a mainstay of print, interactive, and social media for people of every age and occupation."

> – Bill Roberts
> VP-Operations
> Wheelabrator Technologies

"Follow the practical, no-nonsense advice in this book and you will lead a more engaged, committed, and effective team. "

> – Dianne Nilsen, PhD
> Chief Operating Officer
> Questar

"Gordy Curphy and Bob Hogan brought leadership and team development to Husky Energy when I managed the company's organization development portfolio, and this work resulted in Husky winning numerous coveted awards. More recently, the Rocket Model has made its way into the fabric of several other Alberta corporations. This model is simple to teach, learn, and implement, yet powerful in its results."

> – Karen Behar
> President
> To the Core Consulting

Table of Contents

Chapter [1] Introduction to Leadership, Groups, and Teams 1

Chapter [2] Frameworks for Improving Group and Team Performance 13

Chapter [3] Context—What is the Situation? 29

Chapter [4] Mission—What do we need to accomplish? 41

Chapter [5] Talent—Who Is on the Bus? 55

Chapter [6] Norms—What Are the Rules? 75

Chapter [7] Buy-In—Are We All Committed to Win? 97

Chapter [8] Power—What Resources Do We Need? 113

Chapter [9] Morale—Can't We All Get Along? 129

Chapter [10] Results—Are We Winning? 149

Chapter [11] Putting It All Together 163

End Notes 187

References 193

Preface

Since the Italian Renaissance beginning in the 14th century, western civilization has celebrated "The Individual" and his/her personal well-being and achievement. All of our cultural icons are solitary geniuses struggling alone in splendid isolation to produce scientific, artistic, financial, or musical masterpieces. In this view, the great contributions to our culture were produced by individuals, even though the growth of culture itself is often cumulative, the result of one independent genius building on the work of earlier independent geniuses. These themes pervade popular culture as well—heroes of western movies, hard boiled detectives, single-minded explorers are all (usually) men who stand alone against the forces of nature or human wickedness.

Despite the intuitive appeal of the cult of the individual, it is simply wrong as a description of the development of science, business, architecture, military prowess, medicine, or geographical exploration. All significant human accomplishments— space exploration, the building of the pyramids in Egypt and the Great Wall of China—are the result of group effort, of collective coordinated enterprise. The Romans didn't conquer Carthage or Gaul because they were better fighters than the inhabitants; the key to the Roman's success was their talent for social organization. And when the Romans lost this talent for coordinated action, they were overrun by the "barbarians".

Despite the obvious importance of collective action, academic psychologists only began to study group and team dynamics sometime after World War II. The stimulus was the need to understand group psychotherapy—a cheaper, more cost effective way of providing therapy—and after WW II, there was substantial demand for mental health services. With this beginning in group therapy, the early team research focused exclusively on group processes and group dynamics and tried to understand group behavior at the level of the group itself. As a result, it wasn't until the late 1980s that researchers began to investigate the determinants of group or team effectiveness—what is required in terms of team structure and dynamics for a team to perform at a high level.

The question of the nature of team effectiveness becomes even more important when we realize that people evolved as groups of living animals in a context of intense competition for survival. There was conflict within human groups, as individual members competed for status (as they still do), and there was conflict between the human groups as they competed for territory and the food supplies contained therein. Some historians have argued that World War II was all about: (1) the Japanese conquering territory outside the Japanese homeland for the purposes of agriculture; and (2) the Germans pushing east for *lebensraum*—territory for agriculture to feed their population. In both cases, however, the territory was already occupied; hence the conflict. Across the course of history, competition between groups has been deadly serious; in most cases the losers were killed, frequently eaten, and in any case the losers always disappeared from the gene pool. In short, human history can be framed in terms of the competition between groups, and the effective groups prevailed.

It is a short conceptual step from envisioning the competing groups in human prehistory to thinking about the modern business environment. Most organizational theorists think of the rise and fall of business organizations in terms of structural factors like business cycles, geography, and the environment—factors external to the organization over which the members have little control. But it is also possible to analyze the components of organizations that contribute to or detract from their effectiveness. However, at the tops of business organizations (and governmental entities), people are mostly preoccupied with politics and individual political survival; consequently, it is difficult to get policy makers to pay attention to issues of competent team management. But the island nation of Singapore provides a stunning example of what happens when policy makers run a country like an effective business.

Imagine now that we clearly understand the structures and processes needed to build and run an effective team or group; the next question concerns how to put that understanding in place to fix existing teams or groups. Precisely this question confronts every new manager in every public and private sector organization in the world and this book provides the answer to the question. The book is the product of years of reading, research, reflection, and operational experience. The lessons it contains are invaluable—but only if a person is interested in shaping a team in ways that will allow it to outperform the competition. The lessons of the book do not concern how to make individuals feel better about themselves—readers can consult Facebook and Twitter for that help. Rather, the lessons concern how to keep a business functioning effectively, or a team performing at a high level. Mostly in life, if one's business, or government, is functioning effectively, people will then have the time and money to worry about their individual self-esteem. But if one is forced to live in failed social organizations, then there will be little time to worry about self-esteem. In short, this book provides answers to some of the most important questions in human affairs.

– Robert Hogan
Amelia Island, Florida

[1]

Introduction to Leadership, Groups, and Teams

The isolated and forbidding Auckland Islands lie three hundred miles south of New Zealand. For centuries, mariners have struggled to navigate these treacherous waters. Ships that sailed too close to these formidable islands were usually grounded on the shallow reefs by the fierce sub-Antarctic winds that ravaged the shoreline. The ships capsized and the crew typically drowned. Those few souls who did manage to make it to the shore most likely died of exposure and starvation; however, the fortunate few who managed to survive did so in dreadful conditions. In *Island of the Lost*, a story of leadership and teamwork, Joan Druett recounts the tale of two parties shipwrecked on opposite sides of the main island in 1864.[1]

The first group, a party of five led by Captain Thomas Musgrave of England, worked together in a coordinated effort to survive. Over 20 months, using material salvaged from their ship, they built a cabin, found food, rotated cooking duties, nursed one another, made tools, tanned seal hides for shoes, built a bellows and a furnace, and built a boat which they used to sail to safety.

Meanwhile, 20 miles away on the other side of the island, a Scottish ship led by Captain George Dalgarno went aground, and 19 men made it safely to shore. However, Delgarno became severely depressed and went mad while his crew rapidly descended into anarchy and cannibalism. A sailor named Robert Holding tried to encourage the others to act together in order to build shelter and find food, but the rest of the crew threatened to kill and eat him. After three months, only three men were alive to be rescued.

Many academics think there is no such thing as leadership and that the fate of teams and collectives somehow unfolds willy nilly. However, if there is no such thing as leadership, then there can be no such thing as a successful team because leadership and team performance are inextricable. Musgrave's and Dalgarno's stories demonstrate that leadership and team performance have life and death consequences. History is full of similar examples, from Ernest Shackleton's trip through the Arctic to save his crew[2] to Vinegar Joe Stilwell's March out of Burma which saved 100 soldiers and nurses from torture and death by the invading Japanese army.[3]

We have all been on teams that have had talented people yet somehow failed miserably, while other less talented teams succeeded despite long odds. Effective teamwork is a critical part of every significant human achievement. Neil Armstrong could never have set foot on the moon without the support of his team of astrophysicists, engineers, mechanics, programmers, politicians, etc. Harriet Tubman relied on her massive network of friends and supporters to keep the Underground Railroad on track. Nonetheless, Americans tend to glorify individual talents and accomplishments, while drastically underestimating the amount of cooperation needed to achieve anything of note.[4] Because groups and teams are the means by which most things get done in organizations, being able to get people to work together more effectively can be the difference between winning and losing in today's competitive business environment.

The purpose of this chapter is to help leaders understand the nature of effective groups and teams. We begin by discussing the pervasiveness of groups in organizations, and the reasons why they often fail to perform well. We then describe the differences between groups and teams. Although the differences tend to be more a matter of degree than substance, some of them can have profound implications for leaders. Furthermore, we review several myths and misunderstandings about team dynamics that can interfere with a leader's ability to efficiently delegate work to others.

Groups Are Commonplace, but Good Teamwork Is Rare

Over a lifetime, most people spend a substantial amount of time taking part in various groups and teams. If a person added up the number of work groups, task forces, steering committees, project teams, athletic teams, volunteer groups, and community or religious out-reach organizations that he or she has been or is currently part of, the total might run into the hundreds. Nonetheless, most people would say that being in an effective team is a rare experience. Why is it that people spend so much time playing or working in groups that are not productive, effective, or cohesive? This is a fascinating question, and our studies of hundreds of groups and teams show that the most common reasons why teams fail are as follows:

The Top 10 Reasons Why Groups and Teams Fail

1. Misunderstanding the team context.

2. Lacking a common purpose or goal.

3. Issues with team composition.

4. Bad followership.

5. Poor meeting, decision-making, and communication processes.

6. Favoritism.

7. Differing levels of commitment.

8. Shortfalls in resources (funding, equipment, or authority).

9. Personal animosity and interpersonal conflict.

10. Being unable to achieve superior results.

1. *Misunderstanding the team context.* All groups and teams operate in a context that is defined in terms of the internal and external constituencies that affect them. Some of these include customers, competitors, parent organizations, suppliers, government regulators, and organizational functions (i.e., marketing, sales, IT, HR, etc.). We once worked with a software development team whose members had very different assumptions about their customer needs and their competitors. These assumptions were never explicitly articulated, causing team members to develop product features that were often misaligned with customer needs. Subsequently, the team suffered from feature creep, quality problems, and late releases until the leader held a discussion challenging the assumptions team members held about their key constituencies.

2. *Lacking a common purpose or goal.* Groups that lack a common purpose, clearly defined goals, and an explicit set of metrics to evaluate progress

are unlikely to achieve meaningful results. In many cases, individual team members have specific personal goals but only vague ideas about what their team is trying to achieve. For example, we consulted with a human resources leadership team that lacked team goals or metrics. Team members worked hard to accomplish their individual goals but showed little interest in helping one another succeed. The morale and performance of the team were far lower than that of other teams simply because the leader failed to get the members to agree on a set of common goals and metrics.

3. *Issues with team composition.* Some teams have too many people; others too few. Some team members have poorly defined roles, and some team members lack the essential skills needed for the team to be successful. Other teams are composed of people who were chosen for political reasons rather than talent considerations. Leaders who do not align team members' talents to their teams' needs and goals create ineffective teams.

4. *Bad followership.* Although team leadership captures much more attention, team followership is also crucial for team success. Good followership concerns the effectiveness with which team members identify problems, propose solutions, and follow through on decisions. Poor followers are unable or unwilling to do one or more of these things. We once conducted an off-site meeting for an audit leadership team where one of the key team members whined, moaned, and made it clear that she was truly unhappy to be at the session. This person was an energy vampire until she and her team leader had a "come-to-Jesus" coaching session. Sometimes there are moments when team leaders need to play sheriff to insure that everyone is pulling in the same direction.

5. *Poor meeting, decision-making, and communication processes.* Many teams suffer from a lack of meeting discipline, bad decision-making processes, and poor communication flow. The power of these debilitating bad habits was perfectly demonstrated when we worked with an executive team whose CEO complained about his staff's poor participation in team meetings. On closer inspection, we realized that his team meetings consisted of a series of back-to-back presentations allowing no time for breaks or discussions. The CEO sat at the front of the room to better hear the presenters while the remaining members of the executive team sat behind, pecking away at their iPads and Blackberries. We were able to increase the level of participation in subsequent meetings by changing the seating arrangements, redesigning the meeting agendas, and articulating and enforcing expected team member behavior.

6. *Favoritism.* Nothing kills team morale more quickly than the appearance of favoritism. If some team members are not held accountable for breaking team rules and others are punished for relatively minor infractions, it is only a matter of time until the high performers shut down or join other teams. Dysfunctional teams are usually led by leaders who are biased or play favorites.

7. *Differing levels of commitment.* All of us have been on a team where everyone did north-south head nods on critical team decisions and then ignored the decision after the meeting. Also, we know of teams where some people did very little yet took credit for the team's success. Like favoritism, uneven levels of buy-in to team goals, rules, roles, work assignments and processes will quickly erode team cohesiveness and effectiveness.

8. *Shortfalls in funding, equipment, or authority.* Although research shows that many teams squander resources,[b] there are times when they lack the materiel resources or decision-making authority needed to succeed. For instance, we consulted with a group whose job was to determine whether arc-plasma technology was a cost-effective way to dispose of medical waste. Just as the team began working on the problem, the economic recession of 2008-2009 started, prompting the parent company to cut back on its research funding to preserve cash. The subsequent restrictions of funding and resources effectively killed the team.

9. *High levels of animosity and conflict.* We help new teams get launched and existing teams operate more effectively. For the most part, the morale on these teams seems okay, but there are times when we encounter cliques, backstabbing, suspicion, favoritism, political in-fighting, and outright anger. These issues are not limited to lower-level teams; some boards of directors and executive leadership teams show many of the same symptoms. The popular business press describes the Hewlett Packard board as the most dysfunctional in American business—from November, 1992 to September, 2011, the once well-managed HP cycled through and fired five successive CEOs. Throughout this turbulent time, the company lost half its value, and the board continued to quarrel and spy on one another. Most leaders can recognize when team members are not playing well together, but they discount, misdiagnose, or take the wrong actions to deal with this problem.

10. *An inability to achieve superior results.* Because most working groups suffer from at least one of the problems listed above, it is hardly surprising that many fail to meet expectations. This deficiency does not mean that most teams

do not achieve results; rather, they do not perform particularly well when compared to similar teams. The trick here is to find the appropriate comparison groups. Without any benchmarks, it is easy for teams to rationalize their poor performance. By definition, half of the Fortune 500 CEOs are below average, but those in the bottom half of the distribution are still able to explain why they deserve raises. This analogy also holds true for teams.

Lack of effective leadership is the common thread running through these ten reasons why groups and teams fail. Far too often, leaders are either unwilling to take action or do not know how to improve the functioning of their subordinates. Sadly, there are some leaders who simply do not care about the morale or the performance of their teams. Most team dysfunction is due more to a lack of leader know-how than to a lack of motivation. As such, this book is intended to help leaders improve their understanding of group dynamics and provide a roadmap for building high-performing groups and teams.

Groups Versus Teams: Is There a Difference?

To clear up some of the misunderstandings about teamwork, we begin by defining what we mean by groups and teams. So far we have used the terms "team" and "group" interchangeably, but there are actually some differences between these two concepts. We define teams as consisting of three to 25 people who:

- Work toward a common set of goals.
- Work jointly—the team members' performance is interdependent.
- Share common leadership.
- Share a common fate that depends on the performance of the team.
- See themselves as being part of a team with common goals and shared fates.

This definition of teams is somewhat different from the usual definition in three ways. First, according to this definition dyads are not teams. The dynamics between any two people are much simpler than those between three or more people. Second, this definition assumes people share a "mental model" about the teams to which they belong. In other words, they identify themselves as members of a particular team and tend to have common interpretations of events.[6] And third, teams tend to be fairly small—usually less than 25 people. Larger groups may call themselves teams (such as a professional football team), but in reality they are usually groups made up of various sub-teams (the offensive unit, defensive unit, etc.). Common examples of teams might include commercial aircrews, crews of fire fighters, United States Army platoons, product development teams, manufacturing shifts, fast food restaurant crews, research and development teams, and soccer teams. The individuals in each of these examples share common goals, depend on the help of the other team members, share leadership and common fates, and most importantly, identify with their teams.

Groups are clusters of people that do not share these five characteristics to the same extent as teams. A regional sales team responsible for selling insurance and other financial services to local citizens would be a prototypical group. In this so-called team, each sales representative has individual revenue and profitability goals for an assigned geographic territory. An individual's ability to achieve these goals does not depend on what the other sales reps do; instead, it is completely dependent on that person's own performance. Although an individual's effort contributes towards the region's revenues and profitability goals, the region's performance is the sum of each rep's individual efforts. If a regional sales manager wants to increase revenues, then he or she could add reps, expand territories, increase prices, or change the product mix. Requiring the reps to work more closely together would have little, if any, impact on the region's financial performance. As a matter of fact, spending time on team building efforts rather than training individual reps on financial products or sales processes would probably degrade regional sales performance.

This is not to say that leaders play passive roles when managing groups. In fact, the opposite is true. Leaders in charge of groups need to ensure that the members operate under the same assumptions regarding customers and competitors, possess the right skills, stay motivated, share information, have adequate resources, achieve their individual goals, and resolve differences quickly. Contrast these leadership demands with those of a head surgeon of a cardiovascular surgical team. The head surgeon would have many of these same leadership responsibilities, but would need to ensure that his or her fellow surgeons, anesthesiologists, nurse practitioners, and physician assistants identify with the team, practice collaboration, use common work processes, have seamless task handoffs, and share common goals and a common fate as they put stents and pacemakers into patients. Thus, the leadership demands on people in charge of teams are more extensive (and consequently more difficult to master) than the demands on people in charge of groups.

The comparison between a regional sales team and a surgical team represents the two ends of a group versus team continuum. Some collections of people, such as members of an ice hockey team or power plant shift, are more likely to have the characteristics of a team, whereas members of a call center or drivers for an over-the-road trucking company are less likely to show these characteristics. Call center reps hand over customers to other reps and truck drivers depend on dispatchers for guidance, but to a large extent their jobs do not entail the tight interdependence of performance, common goals, and shared fate that is frequently associated with teams.

There are several points worth noting about our distinction between groups and teams. First, we do not assume that teams are necessarily more worthy than groups. The nature of the goals to be accomplished and the work to be performed dictates whether a group or a team approach is the best solution. If members do not share a common goal, operate autonomously, or do not share a common fate, then leaders should manage them as a group. If members have shared goals, need to work interdependently to achieve them, and either win or lose together, then operating as a team is the better approach. The appropriate structure (i.e. groups vs. teams) depends on the task at hand because there are real risks to efficiency, effectiveness, and morale when leaders treat groups like teams and teams like groups. Consequently, it is critical for leaders to determine whether they are in charge of a group or a team and adjust their expectations and style accordingly.

Second, whether a group or a team is the best operational structure depends on the goals to be achieved and nature of the work to be performed. Cohesive, goal-oriented teams usually outperform teams that are less cohesive and goal oriented. The 1980 United States Olympic hockey team is a prime example of how a well-coached but not very talented athletic team can defeat a team with more talent but less cohesion. Leadership plays a critical role in building high-performing teams; consequently, who is in charge and how well he or she plays the role will greatly determine whether teams are winners or losers.

Third, it is not clear where top leadership teams (such as C-Suite, business unit leadership, and functional leadership teams) fall on the group versus team continuum. What happens at the top of a company or unit affects everyone else in the organization. At first glance one might think that these bodies operate more like teams than groups, yet this is not always the case. Some top leaders expect their direct reports to run their respective areas of responsibility, and only interact with their peers on an as needed basis. For example, some CEOs hold their general counsels accountable for managing their law departments and reducing outside legal costs but not for helping devise corporate strategy or improving profitability and share price. Other CEOs hold themselves and their immediate staff responsible for company-wide goals, such as market share, share price, profitability, brand awareness, employee engagement and turnover. Thus, the extent to which top leaders emphasize common goals, interdependent work, or shared fates affects whether their staff operate as groups or teams. Top leaders who manage their direct reports as groups, when they really need to operate as teams (or vice-versa), run the risk of driving these groups and their organizations into the ground.

Fourth, this discussion illustrates an important concept, something that Patrick Lencioni described as the "first team."[7] Is the general counsel's primary allegiance to the CEO's team, or is it to the direct reports and employees of the law department? If it is the latter, the CEO will have a difficult time building a high-performing senior leadership because the direct reports will be more focused on leading their own respective functions than on operating as a high-performing executive team. Unfortunately, many leaders talk about the importance of teamwork but fail to define team goals or hold people accountable for their accomplishments. Those wanting to build high-performing teams need to make sure work is structured so that it fosters teamwork, or they run the risk of doing very little to actually make it happen.

It is important to note that the first-team concept is not limited to teams at the top. For example, a pastor may want to build a high-performing team of outreach volunteers but may have limited success if the team members define their first teams differently. Thus, leaders need to understand the context in which their teams or groups operate. Do leaders have the latitude to set team goals, create joint work goals, and foster a sense of mutual accountability, or are they limited to coordinating and managing the efforts of individual members? By understanding his or her teamwork opportunities and limitations, leaders can set realistic expectations and minimize frustration levels down the road.

Myths and Misunderstandings About Teams: Separating Fact from Fiction

Humans are social animals and spend much of their time working in groups and teams, yet most people don't understand the dynamics of effective teamwork. That is not to say people do not recognize good teamwork when they see it, but knowing what one needs to do in order to get people to work together effectively is a different matter. Some of this confusion is due to common misunderstandings about teams and teamwork, and it is worth pointing out these misunderstandings.

Myth #1: Teams always perform better than individuals. Although we like to think that groups outperform individuals, there are some tasks that are better performed by individuals.[8] Repairing cars, setting up home theaters, and conducting sales calls are examples of individual performance superceding team efforts. Yes, teams of mechanics can work on cars, and companies can endorse eight-legged sales calls, but in many cases this multi-layered approach would degrade the performance of the individuals doing the work. Our default position is to assign work to groups rather than individuals which can lead to redundancies and inefficiencies. Leaders need to look at the nature of the work to be performed and determine the best way to get it done.

Myth #2: Athletic teams are good analogies for business teams. Leaders often use athletic teams as examples for creating high-performing work teams. Given the prevalence and visibility of professional sports teams, these analogies are understandable, but they tend to be misguided. Work teams are nothing like athletic teams. Think about the 2012 Super Bowl Champions – the New York Giants. Many private and public sector leaders (especially in New York) would love their teams to perform like the Giants, but professional athletic teams differ from work teams in four important ways. First, professional athletic teams obsess over talent. Coaches watch college game films to identify talent, and the potential players they choose must participate in combines, mini-camps, training camps, and preseason games before final hiring decisions are made. Many work team members are selected on the basis of their availability and internal politics rather than skill. Second, athletic teams' practice-to-play ratio is something like 100-to-1, whereas work teams spend little, if any, time practicing. Third, professional athletic teams have clear team goals (e.g. win the Super Bowl) and objective measures of success (win-loss records), whereas work teams often suffer from ill-defined goals and metrics. Finally, the challenges and threats facing professional athletic teams (i.e., next week's opponent) are clearly understood, in contrast to the challenges facing work teams which are much harder to anticipate. This does not mean work teams should not borrow some of the best practices of professional athletic teams, but mindlessly applying sports analogies to work teams is not particularly useful.

Myth #3: Corporations are team-oriented. In a list of a company's corporate values, collaboration and teamwork usually appear near the top of the list. Although companies constantly preach the importance of teamwork, many of their processes and systems encourage individualism. Most company's performance management systems are based on individually oriented goals and accomplishments; team goals, contributions, and results typically take a back seat. Likewise, hiring and compensation systems, budgets, and support programs (i.e., IT help desks) are often slanted more towards individuals than groups.

Myth #4: Effective teamwork is common in most organizations. Many people believe that if a group of high-performing individuals is asssembled, those individuals will eventually coalesce into a high-performing team. Unfortunately, we all know examples of work and athletic teams that had the right talent but failed to perform according to expectations. Effective teamwork is a relatively rare occurrence. Although we have all belonged to hundreds of teams, few people have been on high-performing teams. Because most groups and teams use ineffective work processes, squander resources, or suffer from interpersonal conflict, they usually fall short of their goals.

As an overview, Chapter 2 describes four models or frameworks for understanding groups and teams. One of these frameworks is the Rocket Model, which provides leaders with a roadmap for diagnosing and improving team efficiency, effectiveness, and cohesiveness. Many of the reasons that teams fail can be traced back to sub-par performance in one or more components of the Rocket Model. Chapters 3-10 provide more in-depth descriptions and practical activities that leaders can use to improve team functioning in each of the eight components of the Rocket Model. These easily implementable activities have been used with hundreds of real teams, ensuring that readers should not have any problems adapting them for their own use. Although developing effective teamwork is a complicated endeavor, the roadmap and tools provided in this book should help readers make sense out of the challenges they face as team leaders.

[2]

Frameworks for Improving Group and Team Performance

Cofor Corporation, a manufacturing firm, has been in business for more than 100 years. John Cofor started the company to mass-produce rifle and pistol parts for the United States Army. Over time the company expanded into manufacturing parts for a variety of vehicles (e.g. automobiles, planes, trains, etc.). Historically, Cofor's eight manufacturing plants operated as independent business units, each with its own marketing, sales, finance, IT and HR support, and P&L responsibilities.

Although the company averaged five percent growth over the past 20 years and became a $500M business, its major competitors averaged 11 percent growth over the same period. The Cofor Board of Directors, unhappy with the competition's rate of growth and worried about becoming an acquisition target, hired a new CEO to boost growth. The new CEO visited the Cofor plants, studied financial statements and organization charts, reviewed competitive intelligence, met key customers, and began reorganizing the company. He centralized the support functions, shifted P&L responsibilities from the plant managers to his new executive leadership team, and reduced the workforce by ten percent in order to cut redundancies and costs.

The CEO asked Sharon, who has spent her career working at Cofor to join his leadership team as Chief Marketing Officer (CMO) because of her track record in marketing, sales, and operations. He directed Sharon to take a broad view of Cofor's product line and determine which product should be developed, reassigned to different plants, or discontinued. In addition to these responsibilities, Sharon was to play a critical role in product pricing, business acquisition, global expansion, and any product and plant divestitures. Adopting a company-wide product portfolio perspective was a new experience for her, but Sharon felt up to the challenge.

As the CMO, Sharon led a team of six product development directors who helped her manage Cofor's product portfolio. The six development directors, all with at least ten years of experience working at Cofor, were assigned new positions. Each was now responsible for the strategic business plan and mix, pricing, revenues, and profitability of the products in his or her assigned sector (military arms, automotive, etc.). After filling these six positions, Sharon's next challenge was to persuade them to work together effectively. What could she do to synergize the group? Where should she start? How could she determine if the group was making any progress? These puzzling questions can stymie the most enthusiastic leader, but a leader with a roadmap for building a high-performing team can break through roadblocks and navigate detours to find a smooth road to success.

Nightmare Versus Dream Teams

Think about the worst team you have ever been on. Make a clear mental image of this team—who was on it, what the situation was, what the mission was. Now describe the characteristics of this team on a blank sheet of paper. Next, do the same for the best team you have ever been on. If you are like most people, your lists will look something like this:

Nightmare Teams	Dream Teams
Unclear purpose	Well-defined team goals
Ill-defined roles	Clear roles
Wrong people	Right people
Poor decision-making processes	Good decisions
Favoritism	Fair and equitable
No accountability	Mutual accountability
Funding or equipment gaps	Adequate funding
In-fighting and mistrust	Good morale
Exhausting and unpleasant	Invigorating and fun
Losing records or get little done	Winning records or get a lot done

People usually appreciate working on dream teams with their positive characteristics and dislike participating on nightmare teams with the negative aspects. The crucial question is "What should leaders do in order to make effective teamwork happen?" Leaders could more readily answer this question if given the proper resources. This chapter reviews four common models for building high-performing teams: Tuckman's Forming-Storming-Norming-Performing model,[9] Hackman's Inputs-Processes-Outputs model,[10, 11] Lencioni's Five Dysfunctions of a Team,[12] and Curphy's Rocket Model.[13] Although none of these processes has dominated the market, the Rocket Model has several important advantages.

Model or Framework	Comments
Forming-Storming-Norming-Performing	Most groups go through four distinct phases. Leaders need to adjust their behavior to the development phase of the group. Some groups do not go through all four phases.
Inputs-Processes-Outputs	Groups transform raw materials into outputs. Dream, design, and development are critical leader functions. Advanced models too complex to be helpful.
The Five Dysfunctions of a Team	Teams need to work through trust, conflict, commitment, accountability and results. Provides leaders with practical advice. Many recommendations not based on data.
The Rocket Model	Eight components of team effectiveness. Prescriptive and diagnostic model. Leaders given practical advice and team-building activities.

Tuckman's Forming-Storming-Norming-Performing Model

In the mid-1960s, Tuckman reviewed the literature on T-groups, experimental groups of college students, and therapeutic groups, noting that when a group is formed, it passes through four development stages.[14] *Forming* concerns the initial process of getting together. This stage is marked by exchanging social pleasantries, gathering superficial information about others, evaluating each other's possible contribution to the group, and developing trust (usually not much). The group then moves into the *Storming* phase, wherein the members begin arguing about tasks and roles and competing for social status. The defining features of the *Storming* phase are heightened emotions, interpersonal conflict, and no progress. If the group overcomes the issues of goals, roles, and control, it proceeds to the *Norming* phase. In this phase the group's pecking order and individual responsibilities are established. The group begins working on its operating procedures (defining the best ways to get work done, deciding how often to meet, determining when sub-tasks need to be completed, etc.). If the group can agree about ground rules and internal work processes, it advances to the *Performing* stage. In this last phase, members focus on accomplishing group tasks. According to Tuckman, a group must pass through all the stages before it can begin to operate as cohesive team.

Tuckman's Group Development Model

	Storming	Norming	Performing
Polite chatter Probing others Low trust	Posturing Arguing Status Seeking	Rules Processes Meetings	Group tasks Feedback High trust

Tuckman model offers cogent observations. First, the model is a good description of our everyday group experiences. We have all been in groups that started off politely, broke out into conflict over what goals to pursue and methods to use, and eventually settled into a productive rhythm. Second, groups that never progress past the in-fighting and jockeying turn into nightmare teams. Third, according to Tuckman's model, leaders should provide support and encouragement during the first two phases and focus on motivation and goal accomplishment during the latter two group development stages. Providing the wrong leadership in the wrong phases derail the team's performance.

There are three problems with Tuckman's model, however. First, referencing the data he used to develop his model, Tuckman's groups (unlike typical work groups) contained assembled strangers who had to determine what they were to do, who played what roles, etc. Second, other researchers have not been able to replicate Tuckman's stages when watching real work groups. Robert Ginnett observed hundreds of commercial aircrews and surgical teams and reported that not one went through the *Forming* and *Storming* stages of Tuckman's model.[15]

This perception makes sense—airlines would have real problems if each new aircrew argued about who would fly the plane, and hospitals would fail if doctors and nurses constantly argued about which operating procedures to use.

Perhaps the biggest problem with Tuckman's model is the advice it gives leaders. It implies that when group members first get together and fail to coalesce, leaders should gather everyone around a campfire and sing "Kumbaya." Leaders who provide support during the Forming and Storming phases only provide temporary relief for the underlying problems, which often makes matters worse.

Likewise, waiting until groups have worked through their issues before discussing goals, roles, and work processes usually leads to mediocre performance and wasted time. For these reasons, Tuckman's model may not be particularly helpful to Sharon, the CMO we introduced at the beginning of this chapter.

Inputs-Processes-Outputs Model

Another popular framework is the Inputs-Processes-Outputs model promoted by Richard Hackman.[16] *Inputs* refer to the raw materials available to the group or team. Inputs include the number of team members; the budget, facilities, and equipment available to the team; the organization's culture, IT and HR systems; and government regulations, customer needs, and suppliers. A leader's ability to influence team inputs varies considerably—some components he can control; others he will have to reconcile.

Processes are the activities in which teams engage and the systems they use. Common process factors include strategies for doing the work, the level of effort and skills required, and the effects of group dynamics.

Outputs are the results of a group's work. A football team may score 24 points, a regional sales group may generate $4,000,000 in monthly sales, and a plant leadership team might cut costs by 12 percent; by themselves, however, these results are meaningless. The big question is how do these results stack up against those of comparable teams? Or, do they meet the customers' needs? Hackman argues that group effectiveness should be evaluated according to which outputs meet customers' needs and help individual group members grow and develop.

Hackman's Inputs-Processes-Outputs Model

Inputs	Processes	Outputs
Purpose # of members Budget Customers	Work strategies Level of effort Skills Group dynamics	Group results Customer sat Member sat Enhanced skills

Hackman believes a leader needs to create the conditions necessary for team success. This environment is achieved through three critical functions of team leadership: dream, design, and development.[17,18,19] The dream function concerns ensuring that groups or teams have a clear vision about where they are going. The leader usually creates the vision; however, sometimes it can arise from conversations with the group. Either way, having a clear vision is essential for success. Design includes devising approaches for getting work done, selecting the right team members with the right skills, obtaining necessary equipment, sorting out roles and work handoffs, etc. Although team design is important for team success, many leaders overlook this component. Development involves finding solutions that increase the effectiveness of group interaction. In order for the development function to be fulfilled, leaders must adopt a continuous improvement mindset towards team processes, work handoffs, and skill development.

The Inputs-Processes-Outputs model is useful in several ways. First, the model is intuitive: raw materials go in, groups work on them, and then groups generate outputs. Second, the model pays more attention to the variety of internal and external factors that affect teamwork than Tuckman's model does. Third, unlike Tuckman's approach, the model clearly describes what leaders need to do (i.e., dream, design, and develop) in order to help their teams become more effective. Finally, the model proposes that leaders can improve performance by coaching the team through their design issues without waiting for evidence that the team is not performing effectively.

Nonetheless, Hackman's model has a major limitation. Some of the advanced versions of the Inputs-Processes-Outputs model are so complex that they look like posters for the "This is Your Brain on Drugs" campaign.[20] If Sharon (our CMO introduced at the start of the chapter) wants to use an advanced version of the model, she will need the help of an experienced consultant, something that many organizations can't afford. Leaders usually have limited time and money; therefore, they need roadmaps that they can use without any help from consultants. The next two models better fit this bill.

The Five Dysfunctions of Teams

Patrick Lencioni's book, *Five Dysfunctions of a Team: A Leadership Fable*[21] provides a third roadmap for building a high-performing team. To illustrate the five key reasons why teams fail, Lencioni uses the story of a fictitious CEO who has to turn around an ineffective leadership team. Like Tuckman, Lencioni describes a sequence of stages with which leaders need to deal (Dysfunction I, II, III, etc.). The first stage, *Dysfunction I: Absence of Trust*, is characterized by teams that won't admit mistakes or offer help, who jump to conclusions, assume negative intent, hide shortcomings, and focus on protecting their reputations. Leaders can help teams progress through Dysfunction I by demonstrating vulnerability and having team members participate in various trust-building exercises such as sharing personal histories or assessment results, providing peer feedback, or participating in outdoor team-building events.

Teams in the *Dysfunction II: Fear of Conflict* stage are characterized by boring meetings, false harmony, and avoidance of controversial topics. Groups in Dysfunction II experience high levels of conflict that is often expressed as passive-aggressive behavior and covert backstabbing. Leaders can help their teams deal with this dysfunction by raising controversial topics and focusing discussions on issues rather than team members; these exchanges can be arenas to create a sense of 'team-spirit' whereby no member is being vilified/victimized.

The *Dysfunction III: Lack of Commitment* stage is typified by analysis-paralysis, frequent reexaminations of past decisions, a pervasive need for consensus, and ambiguity about team direction and priorities. Leaders can help teams work though these issues by making more autocratic decisions, setting decision deadlines, pushing for closure, and resisting the temptation to revisit decisions.

Lencioni's Five Dysfunctions of Teams

Dysfunction V:
Inattention to Results

Dysfunction IV:
Avoidance of Accountability

Dysfunction III:
Lack of Commitment

Dysfunction II: Fear of Conflict

Dysfunction I: Absence of Trust

Teams in *Dysfunction IV: Avoidance of Accountability* are characterized by mediocrity, favoritism, resentment, missed deadlines, and lack of consequences for poor performance. Although leaders must demonstrate some authority, Lencioni believes that truly effective teams are able to police themselves.

Dysfunction V: Inattention to Results is defined as teams that underperform compared to their counterparts and whose members are focused on their own careers rather than achieving team success. Lencioni suggests that this underachievement can be cured by focusing on team goals, setting team performance rewards, regularly monitoring results, and, most importantly, teaching team members how to win.

Lencioni's model provides useful insights about team dynamics and has some advantages over the other models. The model is straightforward, identifies many of the reasons why teams fail, and offers practical advice on how to build high-functioning teams. Lencioni also deserves credit for pointing out the following: (1) the importance of the "first team" (as described in Chapter 1); (2) the need for leaders to teach teams how to win; (3) the recognition of time wasted avoiding conflict; and (4) the cascading effect of leadership team dynamics. The simplicity of the Five Dysfunctions model, key insights, and 'touchy-feely' approach to team building make it popular among human resource professionals and team consultants.

Nonetheless, Lencioni's book is explicitly a work of fiction; it is not based on research and its practical recommendations lack empirical support. For example, when the trust level among team members is low, Lencioni recommends that leaders put them through a series of personal disclosures and outdoor experiential exercises. However, there is little likelihood that these activities can build trust in dysfunctional work teams. It is more likely that leaders of low-trust teams will invite the members to a paint ball outing but be the only persons with guns. According to Katzenbach and Smith, the only effective method for teams to build trust and cohesion is to do real work,[22] and sharing the Myers-Briggs Type Indicator[23] results do not constitute real work.

Similar problems afflict the four other dysfunctions. Dysfunctions III and IV concern lack of commitment and accountability. Although these are important issues, what exactly are team members supposed to be committed to and accountable for? Blind commitment and accountability might have worked for the German SS in World War II, but it won't work for modern-day work teams. People need to understand the team goals, their roles, and the rules of engagement before they will commit to and feel accountable for team success. Similarly, Lencioni suggests that teams must work through Dysfunctions I-IV before they can worry about results; however, few work teams can afford to wait for developmental dynamics to unfold.

Nonetheless, the model's simplicity, the insights it provides into group dynamics, and the practical advice on how to build teams are important positive features. The model's usefulness, however, is limited by its lack of empirical support and poorly thought-out recommendations. Sharon, our novice CMO, will need sound research data and effective problem-solving guidance to help her teams succeed.

The Rocket Model

Our work with hundreds of public and private sector groups and teams across the United States and Europe suggests that leaders need a practical, well-researched model for team building.[24, 25] The Rocket Model provides leaders with sound practical advice on how to improve group and team dynamics. The model is both descriptive and prescriptive—it can be used to diagnose team functioning and make specific recommendations regarding how to launch new teams or to improve the performance of more established teams. The Rocket Model consists of eight components.

Context: What is the situation?

Teams do not operate in a vacuum. The first step in building high-performing teams is gaining agreement on team context. Team members often have different assumptions about their customers, suppliers, or competitors; these differences can destroy morale and undermine efficiency and effectiveness. It is important to note that team members' assumptions are implicit—team members rarely articulate their assumptions about key constituencies. To make the implicit explicit, leaders should help team members understand their key customers, competitors, regulatory agencies, vendors, parent organization and then agree on the key assumptions for each constituency. Gaining agreement on team context makes it easier to determine the team's purpose and goals and to align team member's efforts.

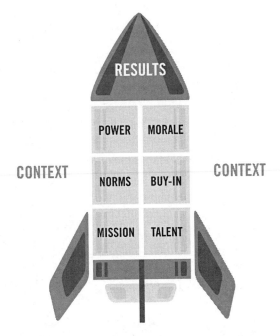

Mission: What do we need to accomplish?

Teams that lack clear goals are like rockets with maximum thrust and no direction—their members go off in all directions with no common purpose. Leaders who help their teams identify key goals, adopt metrics and benchmarks, and regularly review progress have teams that operate at higher levels than those with unclear goals. *Mission* is the most important component in the Rocket Model; team goals should determine who is on the team (Talent), the rules by which the team operates (Norms), the level of commitment and equipment needed (Buy-In and Power), team cohesiveness (Morale), and the outcomes to be obtained (Results).

Talent: Who is on board the ship?

The *Talent* component of the Rocket Model proposes that teams need the right number of people with the right skills to accomplish their goals. The number and types of people needed varies according to the goals; if goals change, then so do the skills needed by the members. Possible reasons for *Talent* failure are the team (1) does not have the right number of people (too many people can be as problematic as too few), (2) does not have people with the right skills, (3) lacks clearly defined roles, and (4) has people who are not team players. Getting the right number of people with the right skills on the team seems relatively easy, but many leaders recruit team members based more on their availability or in-house politics than on talent.

Bad team members are called "team killers." Consider Terrell Owens, a fabulously talented American football player whose bad attitudes and egocentrism destroyed the functioning of every team on which he played. The San Francisco 49ers recruited him out of college in 1996 as the successor to their Hall of Fame receiver, Jerry Rice. However, Owens' attitude wrecked team morale, and he was subsequently traded to the Philadelphia Eagles in 2004. Although warned that Owens would be a problem, the Eagles' coach Andy Reid said that the Eagles' culture was so strong that it could easily absorb a potential troublemaker like Owens. Reid was wrong—Owens destroyed the coherence of the Eagles and the team's performance. He was traded to the Dallas Cowboys in 2006, where he was again a major team killer and was unconditionally released in 2009. Owens' insubordination and selfishness completely outweighed his physical gifts. Team killers sap team cohesiveness and morale, so the issue is simple: they must either play nicely or be replaced.

Norms: What are the rules?

Norms are the unwritten rules that team members follow at work. One team norm concerns seating arrangements. People typically take the same seats at team meetings. Although seating is not usually assigned, this norm becomes clear as soon as someone sits in another's seat. Like seating arrangements, there are a number of implicit, informal rules that influence team member behavior.

Norms for greeting, meeting, seating, communicating, deciding, and accomplishing tasks develop whenever people work together. Although team members may not discuss these topics, they profoundly impact team cohesiveness and performance. A key question for leaders is whether their teams' current set of norms help or hinder team success. If it is the latter, then leaders can work with their teams to identify the norms currently in place and set new ones. High-performing teams set explicit norms for meetings, communication, decision-making, and accountability—norms that are aligned with team goals.

Buy-In: How do you drive engagement and committment?

Buy-In can be defined as the level of engagement and commitment team members assign to the team goals, roles, and work processes. When teams have high levels of commitment, all the members play hard, observe team norms, and contribute to team success. When teams have mixed engagement, some members carry the load and others merely go along for the ride. The degree to which members faithfully carry out team decisions is a good way for leaders to assess team buy-in.

Leaders can foster team member engagement in three ways. One is to outline a compelling team mission because teams tend to work harder when their goals are related to something they believe in. Second, leaders can involve team members in the creation of team goals, roles, and norms. Third, nothing kills buy-in more quickly than perceptions of favoritism; thus, leaders foster commitment by holding everyone accountable to the same standards.

Power: What resources are needed?

All teams have material needs—e.g., funding, office space, hardware and software systems, specialized equipment, etc. Team goals determine these requirements; for example, football teams and pharmaceutical R & D teams require different equipment and facilities. Nonetheless, research shows that many teams simply squander their resources.

The leader's role in the *Power* component is to help their teams identify, acquire, and efficiently use their resources. A potentially tricky *Power* problem occurs when teams lack adequate decision-making authority. In such situations, leaders must ensure that team members understand what is in and out of scope while avoiding authority creep. Leaders can strictly stay within the authoritative bounds dictated by their superiors, or they can lobby for additional authority—a risky approach that may limit career opportunities. If additional decision-making authority is needed, a leader should choose an approach based on the Context, Mission and Norms of the team.

Morale: Can't we all get along?

Morale is one of the more visible components of the Rocket Model—it is relatively easy to tell when teams are playing Dysfunctional Family Feud. Nonetheless, leaders need to remember that polite teams tend to achieve polite results, and that high-performing teams have a fair amount of conflict. Unlike dysfunctional teams, high-performing teams get their conflicts on the table, focus on the issues at hand (not on other team members' faults), and develop ways to resolve disagreements. Thus, conflict within a team is not always bad. If team members constructively challenge the status quo, creative solutions can be found. However, many leaders pretend conflict doesn't exist, or they deal with it by using superficial team-building activities such as golf outings or barbecues—activities that don't address the causes of the conflict and yield only temporary morale improvement.

Results: Are we winning?

The *Results* component is the outcome of the Rocket Model. That is, good team results depend on team members sharing assumptions, being committed and working toward team goals, having clear roles and the right skills, adhering to agreed-upon norms, having the right resources, and effectively managing conflict. Problems in one or more of these components of the Rocket Model usually degrade team performance.

People typically use the win-loss record to evaluate an athletic team's success, but it is sometimes harder to assess a work team's success. The key to evaluating a team effectively is to compare its performance against team goals and the performance of similar teams. Teams that perform well compared with their competitors are successful; conversely, those who can't achieve their goals and perform poorly compared with the competition are unsuccessful.

Some Implications of the Rocket Model

So how could Sharon at Cofor Corporation use the Rocket Model to help her product development directors become a high-performing team? The Rocket Model is prescriptive—it recommends that leaders use an outside-in/bottom's up approach to improve team performance. Accordingly, Sharon's first team meeting should begin by developing agreement on the key external and internal constituencies that affect the team (Context). This evaluation enables the team to set team goals (Mission), clarify roles and responsibilities (Talent), determine an operating rhythm and decision-making process (Norms), and so forth.

But how can leaders use the Rocket Model to improve the performance of teams that have been operating for some time? In such cases, leaders can diagnose their teams' level of functioning by assigning scores to each of the eight components, asking team members to do the same, and consolidating the results. Alternatively, the team can complete a Team Assessment Survey (TAS) II, an on-line survey that provides feedback on the Rocket Model components.[19] An example of some the TAS II results for a Human Resources Leadership Team of a Fortune 500 high-tech firm are presented below:

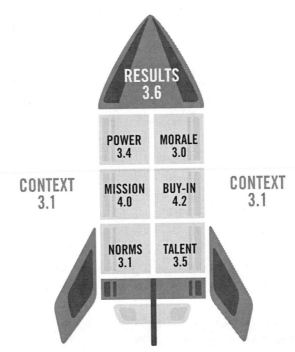

Each component is rated on a one-to-five scale, and these results indicate that the team is doing well on the Mission and Buy-In components but Norms, Context, Morale, Power, Talent and Results are areas that need improvement. Subsequently we designed a two-day off-site for this team that involved reviewing their TAS II results, developing a common set of assumptions about the key constituencies, reviewing the team's goals in light of these assumptions, and establishing better decision-making and accountability norms. This type of assessment provides leaders with the information needed to identify components that are underperforming as well as guidelines to enable their teams to become more efficient (as suggested by the corresponding activities described in Chapters 3-10).

Three other implications of the Rocket Model are worth noting. First, the model gives leaders a practical, research-based framework for building high-performing teams. Second, the assessments, exercises, and activities found in this book have been refined through many years of testing in the field and can be used with any group. And third, the Rocket Model can improve the performance of both groups and teams. Although developing buy-in to common goals may be less relevant for a group, leaders can improve group performance by ensuring that (a) everyone shares the same assumptions about key constituencies, (b) the right people are in the right roles, and (c) the group has effective norms, adequate resources, and conflict management processes.

The remaining sections of this book explain the Rocket Model, provide in-depth descriptions of its eight components, and suggest activities that leaders can use to improve group and team functioning. These activities are designed to be easily replicated and are supported by many years of real-world use. For seamless implementation, we provide detailed instructions, room arrangements, and time and material requirements for each team-building activity.

[3]

Context—What is the Situation?

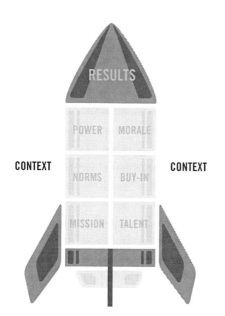

Context Key Points

1. Is this a group or a team?

2. Is this a "first team?

3. Who are the key constituencies?

4. What are our assumptions?

5. How much influence do we have?

6. How does the team add value?

Steve graduated from Indiana University and started working as a junior programmer at the corporate headquarters of Merit Insurance Company. He was bright, ambitious, and worked on several high-profile IT projects that became big successes. He caught the eye of top management and was promoted into a high-potential staff role reporting directly to the CEO. In his new position, he spent two years working on several of the CEO's pet projects and building personal relationships with the company's top leaders.

Because of Steve's apparent potential and his close relationship with the CEO, Merit sponsored him to go to law school. Soon after finishing his law degree, Steve became president of Merit's Colorado division, which had been created after acquiring the Blue Health Company in Denver. Blue Health, an established company, was antiquated, bureaucratic, and had been losing market share and revenues to more aggressive competitors over recent years. Blue Health's declining revenues and sale price made it an attractive acquisition target; however, its customer service, sales, and operations divisions needed fixing. Merit decided that Steve was the perfect person for this job.

At Blue Health, Steve inherited an eight-person executive leadership team with local market and deep functional expertise. Everyone on the team had been with Blue Health for over 20 years, and they got along well. This tightly knit group valued building personal relationships, helping others, encouraging community outreach, and cultivating strong relationships with key brokers, customers, regulators, and other important stakeholders across the state. In the preceding few years, the team rolled out a number of initiatives in an effort to improve revenues, but the measures had little impact on the company's bottom line. The executive team attributed these poor results to the general economic downturn in Colorado and to their competitors' use of unrealistic pricing and actuarial models.

Steve had never been in a formal leadership role before working at Blue Health; however, the culture at Merit emphasized entrepreneurial spirit and a willingness to take risks, along with a mindset that valued results over relationships. As the historian William H. McNeill once noted, when the values of conquering elites are alien to those of the conquered, there will be a lack of sympathy between ruler and ruled.[28] When Steve became a leader in the company, he reflected the philosophy of Merit's "conquering elites" rather than the values of Blue Health's "conquered."

At his first meeting with the leadership team, Steven wanted to assert his authority and make a strong impression; he did 90 percent of the talking, pontificating about his vision for the Colorado division, the importance of Mid-Western values, and the superiority of Merit Insurance Company. He dominated subsequent meetings with the executive leadership team, functional teams, employees, brokers, and customers. His message during these meetings was simple: Blue Health was at an all-time low, and he was there to fix it. Intoxicated with his new position, he argued with and abused anyone who challenged his ideas. Additionally, Steve refused to promote any Blue Health employees during his first year as president. Angered by Steve's attitudes and behavior, the entire executive team and many members of the next two layers of management soon retired or joined other companies.

With the departure of many of the most experienced members of the staff, Blue Health's broker relationships suffered, and the bottom line began to seriously decline. Despite large decreases in new contracts, market share, revenues, and profitability quarter after quarter, Steve avoided taking responsibility and blamed his predecessors for Blue Health's poor performance. Fast forward two years and Steve, who had run the Colorado division into the ground, was removed from the president's position. Steve was not fired for his incompetence but was promoted into a key role at corporate headquarters, an all-too-common fate of popular employees in big corporations.

Context Defined

Steve's failure could be the result of his lack of experience at different leadership levels[29] and his domineering and controlling leadership style. However, his most significant problem was his inability to build a high-performing team. If Steve had been able to work through the various components of the Rocket Model with his executive team, he might have been able to leverage their expertise, build a loyal following, and produce improved results.

Every group and team operates in a specific context. The situation faced by a U.S. Army platoon in southern Afghanistan is different from that faced by a team investigating credit card fraud in South Dakota. Contextual factors critically impact the success or failure of a group, but context is very complicated, and existing research is not very helpful in telling us how it affects team success. The extent to which leaders can control the situational factors affecting their teams and groups varies greatly. Some situational factors can be directly influenced, others can be influenced only indirectly, and many cannot be controlled at all. In such cases, teams should learn how to cope with these factors rather than waste resources changing something that is out of their control.

Key Context Questions

1. Is this a group or a team?

2. Do team members feel this is their "first team"?

3. What are the team's key external and internal constituencies?

4. What are the team's assumptions about these constituencies?

5. How much influence does the team have with these constituencies?

6. How does this team or group add value?

Leaders need to answer several key questions in order to define the context for their teams and groups. Although they can often answer these questions themselves, the team or group will benefit if leaders and members collaborate on the definition as cooperation helps build team/group cohesion and improves interpersonal relationships. Individual members often have answers to key questions but rarely share them with the rest of the group. Therefore, making the *implicit explicit* is a vital task of leadership; groups and teams profit when everyone shares the same understanding about the context, goals, and rules of engagement. This book is designed to help leaders take the implicit assumptions members have about their teams and groups and make those assumptions public and explicit.

Is this a Group or a Team?

The first question leaders and members should ask when trying to define the context is whether they should operate as a group or a team. Teams have common goals, work interdependently, and share common leadership, fates, and identities. Groups, on the other hand, have members with individual goals who do not work interdependently and do not share common fates. Although these differences are a matter of degree, it is essential that leaders and members decide which configuration will obtain the best results. Because of the biased belief that teams are superior to groups, some leaders and members have difficulty determining which approach to use. The decision should be driven by the nature of the work and individual versus common goals, not by the assumptions people have about teams versus groups. Leaders may become discouraged if they believe they are managing a team, but the members are working independently and pursuing their own goals as a group. Many academic and government administrators confront this situation quite often.

Is this the Team Members' "First Team"?

Another issue concerns identifying the primary loyalties of leaders and members. People belong to many different groups and teams; leaders may assume that their direct reports' primary loyalty is to their group when, in fact, it is to some other team. If the leaders or the members identify more closely with another group or team, then leaders are better off treating members as a group, ensuring everyone has the same understanding about context, defining individual goals, providing the necessary skills and equipment, and holding everyone to the same standards of performance. This "first team" discussion can be difficult, but it is better to have it than to try to build a team from members with conflicting loyalties.

What are the Team's Key External and Internal Constituencies?

One way to describe context is in terms of the internal and external constituencies that affect a team or group. A constituency is any entity that influences or is influenced by the group or team's performance. Some common internal and external constituencies are presented in the table below:

External Constituencies	Internal Constituencies
Customers	Boards of Directors
Competitors	Superiors
Suppliers/Vendors	Functions (Legal, IT, Finance, etc.)
Government Regulatory Agencies	Other Internal Teams
Shareholders/Investors	Geographic Dispersion of Team Members
Labor Market	Employees
Industry Analysts	Systems and Processes
Economic Climate	Organizational Culture

The importance of the constituency depends on the group or team. An executive leadership team for a *Fortune* 500 company will largely focus on the board of directors and external constituencies, whereas a human resources team rolling out a new total rewards program will focus on their internal constituencies. Often groups and teams may need to break down their constituencies into smaller segments to better understand their internal and external pressures. For example, they may identify the top five customers, the three biggest competitors, or the two most important internal teams. Leaders and members usually can identify which constituencies are most important for their success. Nonetheless, it is crucial to explicitly identify key constituencies and not assume that everyone is singing from the same hymn sheet.

What are the Team's Assumptions about these Constituencies?

Peter Drucker once noted that flawed assumptions were a major cause of business failures.[30] The same is true for groups and teams. Social psychology reveals that people usually base their actions on their underlying assumptions. Therefore, the more assumptions differ within a group, the more likely peoples' actions will be misaligned. Whereas it may be easy to identify key constituencies, the leaders and members' assumptions about these constituencies are often divergent and poorly specified. It is vital that leaders develop an agreed-upon set of assumptions for key internal and external constituencies. Any discussions arising from identifying assumptions about key constituencies should improve group and team cohesiveness, efficiency, and effectiveness. A step-by-step process for conducting these conversations can be found later in the chapter.

How much Influence does the Team have with these Constituencies?

After developing a common understanding of the group's key constituencies and corresponding assumptions, it is important for the group to consider how much influence it has on the different constituencies. The team may not be able to influence customers, competitors, or the labor market, but it may be able to influence other functional groups, suppliers, or the geographic dispersion of team members. Most groups and teams can benefit by agreeing on the amount of influence they have on their key constituencies. This analysis is important if the group needs additional resources or authority.

How does this Team or Group add Value?

Identifying key constituencies, their underlying assumptions, and the degree to which they can be influenced helps groups and teams determine how they add value to the larger organization. Consider the example of Steve at the beginning of the chapter. He would have been better off if he had begun by working with his team to (1) identify Blue Health's key brokers, customers, competitors, state regulators, local economic conditions, and the culture and key stakeholders at Merit Insurance Company; (2) determine the underlying assumptions for these entities and Merit's business model; and (3) assess the degree to which they could influence these constituencies. After completing these analyses, Steve and his team could have devised strategies for winning business in Colorado and managing the relationships with key stakeholders at Merit Insurance Company.

Conclusion

To summarize, it is important to understand the various context in which teams operate. For example, the context for a television crew filming the Arab uprising is different from that faced by a church fundraising group in rural Alabama. Context determines how a team adds value, who it serves, how much influence it wields, what inter-group interdependencies it has, and how effectively it will get the work done. Consequently, identifying key internal and external constituencies, their underlying assumptions, and the team's ability to influence these entities is an important exercise for any team or group. Key constituencies rarely remain static, so teams must periodically review and update their assumptions, influence ratings, and value propositions to stay efficient and productive.

A key point in this chapter concerns the leader's role in making the implicit explicit. Asking group members to share their rationale for believing in the importance of different constituencies, their assumptions about the situation facing the group, and how much influence the group has will drive alignment and improve team morale. Making the implicit explicit will be a recurring theme as we review the other components of the Rocket Model.

Context Exercises and Activities

The Context Assessment Exercise

The purpose of this book is to provide leaders with a practical roadmap for building more effective groups and teams. The Rocket Model provides this roadmap: the map insets provide more detail about a particular component and the exercises provide specific guidance on how to build better groups and teams. The Context Assessment Exercise has proven very helpful in the following situations:

- Launching new teams and groups.

- Helping new leaders understand established teams.

- Helping geographically dispersed teams fully appreciate the context in which they operate.

- Helping dysfunctional teams and groups determine some of the root causes of conflict.

- Preparing for team or group goal setting.

- Accelerating the on-boarding of new team members.

Context Assessment Exercise for a team or group:

Objective: The purpose of this exercise is to encourage members to share and agree on the context surrounding the group or team.

Room arrangement: A room that can hold everyone on the team, has additional space to do small group breakouts, and has enough wall space to post 10-18 flipcharts.

Time requirement: Usually 90-150 minutes.

Materials requirement: Flipchart paper, markers, masking tape, 3 x 3 Post-It notes, and blank Context Assessment Exercise forms for each member.

Leader Instructions:

1. Explain that groups and teams operate in various contexts and that misaligned assumptions are one of the main reasons for team conflict.

2. Pass out the blank Context Assessment Exercise forms.

3. Explain the concept of key constituencies (internal and external entities that can and do affect teams). These constituencies can include customers, competitors, vendors, funders, functions, other teams, the larger organization, economic conditions, etc.

4. Identify the five to eight most important constituencies to the group. List all the internal and external constituencies on a flipchart and ask team members to vote for the five most important constituencies. At the conclusion of voting, tally up the totals and reconfirm the group's top five to eight constituencies.

5. If the group has more than six people, break into three to four person sub-groups and divide the constituencies among them. Ask the individuals in each sub-group to independently write three assumptions for each assigned constituency on separate Post-It notes. (One assumption per Post-It). Once individuals in a sub-group have finished writing their assumptions, ask them to put all the Post-Its for each constituency on a wall. Sub-groups should discuss commonalities and differences for each assigned constituency and come to agreement on their top three assumptions. The sub-group should then prepare a flipchart that lists the top three assumptions for each of their assigned constituencies and appoint spokespersons.

6. Each sub-group should present its results before the larger group discusses, debates, and modifies the assumptions for each constituency.

7. Once the assumptions have been finalized, work with the larger group to determine the amount of influence the team has on each constituency. Use the following scale to assign the degree of influence:
   +++ = A high degree of influence
   ++ = Moderate influence
   + = Low influence
   0 = No influence

8. Work with the larger group to develop an initial value proposition for the group or team. The group should review the key constituencies, underlying assumptions, and influence ratings and then discuss on how the team adds value. Rather than editing the group's value proposition in this meeting, flipchart the main ideas and assign a sub-group to create a draft value proposition or team charter to be reviewed and edited by all team members. Use another team meeting to get agreement on the final version of the team's value proposition.

9. Assign someone from the group to make an electronic copy of the final set of constituencies, assumptions, and influence ratings to be sent out and reviewed by all team members.

Context Assessment Exercise Form

1. Constituencies	2. Assumptions	3. Influence +++ = High ++ = Moderate + = Low 0 = None	4. Value Proposition

[4]

Mission—What do we need to accomplish?

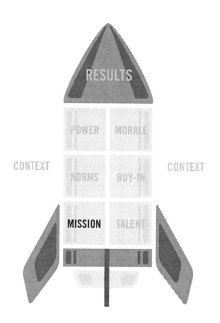

[
Mission Key Points

1. Mission affects the other components.

2. Goals drive behavior.

3. Goals should be specific.

4. Goals should be benchmarked.

5. Focus on the Vital Few.

6. Goals facilitate learning.
]

Smith Financial Services Corporation is a *Fortune* 200 firm that sells health and life insurance, mutual funds, annuities and other financial products. The company has a long and successful history, including several large mutual fund acquisitions and mergers with smaller insurance companies over the past 20 years. Since the Smith philosophy is conservative, the company maintained a healthy balance sheet throughout the 2008-2010 recession by largely avoiding involvement with toxic mortgages and CDOs—unlike many of its competitors.

Rich Hanson joined Smith in the mid-1990s as a first-level manager in the audit division. Identified as a high performer, Rich was promoted to assistant general auditor shortly after the passage of the Sarbanes-Oxley Act in 2002 (a U.S. federal law that seeks to prevent major corporate and accounting scandals such the downfall of Enron). The Sarbanes-Oxley Act encouraged Rich's boss, Luc Robinson, the general auditor, to conduct "scorched-earth" audits that were onerous, time consuming, and corrosive to relationships with the business units. Internal customers felt they were forced to play a high stakes game of "gotcha" while receiving no feedback to help them improve. Luc dismissed the feelings of those being audited—his only priority was to ensure that Smith Financial Services Corporation and its audit committee were in total compliance with the Sarbanes-Oxley Act.

When Luc retired, Rich was promoted to general auditor. He began trying to improve the relationships between the audit division and its internal customers. Additionally, he wanted to restructure his 100-employee division so that it operated more as a team. Luc had ruled the division with an iron fist; however, Rich wanted his direct reports to have more autonomy and bigger roles in the decision-making process. He also wanted to break down the silos between sub-teams and create a more collaborative environment in which employees willingly shared information and resources—a difficult task because the auditors in the different business units and subsidiaries had no desire to collaborate.

After three months on the job, Rich decided to conduct a first-time-ever off-site with his leadership team. When he announced that the off-site was intended to change the division's approach to auditing and improve teamwork, the leadership team became apprehensive. Rich began the off-site by reviewing the current year's audit plan and discussing next year's plan. Because 50 percent of the audits were already late six months into the year, there was a lively discussion about improving their timeliness. The group then reviewed the results of recent customer satisfaction and employee engagement surveys. Although the audit division received high marks for integrity and technical expertise, it received low marks for responsiveness, strategic thinking, business orientation, employee satisfaction and leadership. The leadership team went into a state of denial and insisted that none of these problems was their fault. However, after much debate, they agreed that individual leaders needed to improve the customer relations and employee engagement within their sub-teams before there would be any significant improvements. Later that evening the team went to a baseball game, and over the next two days, the members engaged in several other team-building activities. By the end of the off-site, everyone was feeling good about getting together and anticipating their next meeting.

Mission Defined

The results of this off-site activity are typical. Despite leaders believing that they are building teams, meetings like these are usually a waste of time and money. For example, one of the authors was a partner in a large consulting firm that held quarterly operations meetings. The partners would spend three days covering conference room walls with flipcharts identifying key issues and possible solutions, and making commitments to work harder and smarter. At the next quarterly meeting, the same issues would be identified, and the same commitments would be made. After the third such session, the author told the CEO he did not have a career goal of becoming a monk and would no longer attend the quarterly meetings. When asked about his decision, he said that recreating handwritten documents was something monks did before the invention of the printing press, and future off-sites would be additional episodes in a Groundhog Day charade.

To get their teams operating more effectively, Rich would have been better off using the first off-site to (1) discuss whether direct reports/partners should operate as a team or as a group, (2) identify everyone's "first team," (3) identify the key internal and external constituencies affecting the leadership team, (4) gain consensus on the assumptions about these constituencies and how the team added value, and (5) develop a clear set of team goals, metrics and benchmarks. Subsequent off-sites could then be used to evaluate progress, revise goals, identify barriers, and build action plans to improve team outputs and processes.

Steps 1-4 concern the Context component of the Rocket Model (see Chapter 3); Step 5, however, focuses on the Mission. The management guru Peter Drucker once said that leaders cannot manage something they do not measure.[31] Therefore, if leaders want to make their teams' mission statements or value propositions real, then those statements or propositions need to be defined in terms of measurable team or group goals.

Team and group goals vary with context and purpose. The goals of a group or team (Mission) should drive

- its size, skill requirements, roles and responsibilities (Talent),
- its meeting frequency, decision-making, and communication needs (Norms),
- the level of commitment needed (Buy-In),
- resource needs (Power),
- espirit de corps and conflict resolution (Morale),
- and the desired outcomes (Results).

Team and group goals define what is to be accomplished, when it needs to be accomplished, and how to know when it has been accomplished. Therefore, leaders must spend time developing well-defined goals and metrics for their groups and teams if they want to succeed.

Goals also determine whether members operate as a group or a team. If members do not work together or share common identities or fates, then they need to operate as a group. Conversely, they may need to operate as a team if the members' fates are tied to the accomplishment of the same goal and collaboration is necessary for success. Having well-defined goals, metrics, and benchmarks improves both team and group performance because everyone knows what is required. However, the decision to operate as a team or group depends on how the goals are defined.

Setting goals requires answering some key questions. The remaining sections of this chapter are intended to shed more light on five important questions pertaining to group and team goals.

What Is the Relationship between Goals and Behavior?

The social science literature provides substantial evidence showing that goals drive behavior. If leaders want to change the behavior of a team, they need to change the team's goals. The idea that individual goals drive individual behavior and team goals drive team behaviors seems intuitive, but leaders still expect teamwork by setting individual goals and rewarding individual performance. Steven Kerr calls this the folly of rewarding "A" while hoping for "B", a disconnect that happens all the time.[32] For example, managers often reward account executives for hitting certain revenue targets, and to be successful, the executives must make sales calls, set up meetings, submit proposals and close deals. As a matter of course, they usually avoid activities that interfere with their work routine. Sales managers may want account executives to share ideas and work together, but the executives may see collaboration as a waste of time. Leaders need to understand that their members' behaviors are reinforced by how they are rewarded. If leaders reward the wrong behaviors, then teams or groups will never achieve their goals.

Key Mission Questions

1. What is the relationship between goals and behavior?

2. How specific should goals be?

3. What is the difference between benchmarking and navel-gazing?

4. How many goals should a group or team have?

5. What is the relationship between goals and learning?

How goals are measured also impacts behavior. For example, a major airline set a goal of improving customer loyalty. The airline asked customers for satisfaction ratings on post-flight surveys. However, 15 of the 20 survey questions concerned the kiosks at the check-in counters (e.g. Were the kiosks clean, easy to use and accessible?). Few frequent flyers use kiosks, and there were no survey questions about parking, security, the boarding process, flight attendants, pilots, flight delays, the airplane or other factors that affect customers' flying experience. Although the survey results led to better kiosks—which were soon rated as among the best in the business—customer satisfaction ratings remained low. The lesson learned: Goals drive behavior, but goal measurement must be pertinent and broad in scope.

This example highlights the importance of evaluating progress with the right measures which include both leading and lagging indicators.[33] Lagging indicators provide a picture of past performance—market share, financial performance, product quality or quantity, and number of customers signed up over the last quarter. Leading indicators—customer satisfaction ratings, team member engagement ratings and turnover, or the number of website hits—provide forward-looking information. Ideally, leaders should use both leading and lagging indicators to evaluate progress.

So far we have noted that (1) team goals drive team behavior, (2) the measures used to define goals matter, and (3) goals should include both leading and lagging indicators. It is more difficult to create measurable goals for some teams than for others. For instance, it is often easier to set goals involving sales, customer service, procurement and finance than it is for human resources, public and government relations, legal and research and development. Nonetheless, if leaders want their direct reports to operate as a team, then they need to set team, as opposed to individual, goals. Otherwise they run the risk of rewarding "A" while hoping for "B".

Should Goals Be General or Specific?

Academics have furiously debated whether groups and teams perform better when they are told to do their best or when they are assigned specific goals. The research overwhelmingly supports the latter.[34, 35] The problem with assigning members do-your-best goals is that it is hard to know how much effort is needed, whether team members are making progress. and what methods achieve the best results. Public schools provide a classic example. School districts spend billions of dollars each year in efforts to improve student achievement and attainment. However, it is not

SMART Goals	
Specific	Goals should target a single, specific outcome. Instead of having a single goal of "improving margins and customer satisfaction," teams should have one goal for margins and another for customer satisfaction.
Measurable	Goals should also include the metrics or methods to be used to evaluate success. Common measures might include revenue, production indicators, customer turnover, safety indicators, etc. All team goals should be defined in terms of quantity, quality, timeliness, and/or cost. It is likely that multiple team goals and measures need to be used to direct team performance.
Achievable	Team members must feel the team goals are achievable. Goals that are seen as being too easy or too difficult will fail to energize the people who need to carry them out.
Resourced	There are often many ways to reach a goal, but team members must have the resources they need to get from where they are to where they need to go. These resources may involve time, money, authority, equipment, changes in staffing, changes in priorities, etc.
Time-Bound	Team goals should include final target dates as well as weekly, biweekly, monthly or quarterly reporting dates.

clear whether this money has any significant impact as many districts define their goals as nothing more than improving student achievement. This lack of clarity often results in new programs that waste even more time, effort and resources. School districts would see far better results if they set more specific and measurable goals for student achievement.

The best defined goals are Specific, Measurable, Achievable, Resourced, and Time-bound (SMART—see the above table for a more detailed description). A SMART goal targets a single outcome, includes a metric, is relatively easy to measure, and is bound by time constraints (see below for a comparison between a SMART goal and a vague goal). For instance, marketing teams can decide if they are making progress or need to find better methods for generating leads if they set SMART versus vague goals. By defining carefully the team's goal, leaders can focus team efforts and reduce wasted time and resources.

Vague Goal	Improve lead generation.
SMART Goal	Generate at least 150 qualified leads per month by January 1st, 2014.

What Is the Difference Between Benchmarking and Navel-Gazing?

Another important aspect of goal setting concerns benchmarking. Ask yourself how many times you have carried out a task and felt you were simply shooting in the dark with no idea how well you were doing? Research shows that team members who are given regular feedback on goal progress usually achieve better results because the individuals understand what they are doing right and how they can improve.[36, 37] Thus, teams and groups should set performance criteria for their SMART goals and periodically evaluate their progress. Group and teams can use the following four categories and corresponding color-coding scheme to judge goal progress:

= Exceeding Target

= On Target

= Caution – Near/Below Target

= Well below Target

Adding these four categories to the marketing team's SMART goal of increasing leads produces the following:

SMART Goal				
Generate at least 150 qualified leads per month by January 1st, 2014.	<130	131-149	150-169	>170

When leaders set criteria for goal performance, they need to understand the difference between navel-gazing and external benchmarking. Navel-gazing involves teams and groups comparing their performance to themselves. The criteria set for the marketing team's lead generation is navel-gazing because the marketing team intends to compare its monthly performance against itself. Although-navel gazing can be useful, teams can learn much more by comparing themselves with other groups and teams. As an example, an executive leadership team could adopt the goal of becoming the best place to work and might see year-over-year improvements in employee satisfaction ratings, yet still rank in the bottom quartile compared to others in the industry. Similarly, product development groups can meet all their internal metrics and still have poor reviews by *Consumer Reports* or industry analysts. Therefore, the acid test for leaders is to determine how their groups and teams compare with the competition. Setting goals that include external benchmarks is the only way gather this information. Groups often struggle to identify external benchmarks, but not doing so risks winning battles but losing the war.

How Many Goals Should a Group or Team have?

How many goals do a group or a team need? Unfortunately there is no right answer to this question. Although groups or teams rarely have too many goals, the specificity of the goals is the important thing. Nonetheless, once leaders understand the concept of benchmarked goals, they can apply the standard to virtually every aspect of a group or team's performance.

The number of SMART-B goals set depends on what the teams are trying to do and the kind of leading, lagging and benchmarking information they have available. The executive leadership teams of many *Fortune* 500 companies may create and track 50-100 SMART-B goals for customer segments, products and services, research and development, business development, marketing and sales activities, financial indicators, market share, industry analyst ratings, suppliers, employee productivity and satisfaction, turnover, succession planning, etc. Although these goals help top leaders understand the business, some goals are more important than others. Every team has a Vital Few—a handful of SMART-B goals needed to keep members focused on what is needed for success.

It is usually easy for teams and groups to determine their Vital Few—and, when asked, the members can usually tell what they are. However, there are situations when it can be difficult to determine the Vital Few. For example, a sales group may think monthly revenues are their number-one priority, but local market share might be a better indicator of performance. At the same time, their boss may be more interested in margins than revenues. Each goal drives different account executive behaviors—some of which may conflict. Of course, the sales group could adopt all three goals as their Vital Few, but this combination would lead to paralysis.

Mission: Example of a Team Scorecard

Team SMART Goals	Benchmarks				Results by Month											
					Jan	Feb	Mar	Apr	May	Jun	Jul	Aug	Sep	Oct	Nov
1. *Generate $3.6M in annual sales by Dec 2014 (300k/month).* *	<200	201-300	301-400	<401	On Target	On Target	Caution	On Target							
2. *Generate 1.2M in EBIT by Dec 2014 (100k/month).* *	<80	81-100	101-120	<121	Well below	Well below	Well below	Well below							
3. Increase local market share from 28 to 42% by Dec 2014.	<28	29-42	43-45	<46	Caution	On Target	On Target	Caution							
4. Reduce branch turnover from 24% to 5%/month by Dec 2014.	>24	23-5	4-2	>2	Well below	Caution	On Target	On Target							
5. Increase customer satisfaction ratings from 72% to 85% by Dec 2014.	<72	72-85	85-90	<90	On Target	Exceeding	Exceeding	Exceeding							

|||| = Exceeding Target   ///// = Caution – Near/Below Target   Note: Goals showing * are the Vital Few.

≡ = On Target   ⊠ = Well below Target

What is the Relationship Between Goals and Learning?

Teams and groups operate in environments where customers defect, new competitors emerge, suppliers miss shipments, and members join other teams. Teams and groups react differently to these changes depending on the personalities of the leader and the members, the availability of resources, etc. Some operate in a crisis-du- jour mode and react strongly to each and every change; others see the changes as new challenges and take them in stride. The primary difference will be the degree to which the Vital Few goals are used as filters to assess the changes.

Although situational events may seem serious, if they don't impact the Vital Few, then they can be ignored. Teams that lack the Vital Few see even minor changes as major threats and burn people out with constantly shifting priorities.

In addition, teams with SMART-B and Vital Few goals are proactive rather than reactive. Understanding the team's goals and regularly reviewing team performance against benchmarks helps members devise methods to improve performance. Specified goals also help teams celebrate success; teams or groups with poorly defined goals can never win because they don't really know what they are trying to accomplish. For example, how can a school district know if student achievement is improving unless it sets goals and benchmarks for graduation rates, test scores, achievement gap scores, etc.?

Helping teams to evaluate the importance of unexpected changes, to be proactive, and to celebrate success are benefits of SMART-B and Vital Few goals. An additional bonus is that groups and teams continue to learn and improve. Regularly assessing team performance against goals and benchmarks allows teams to determine whether (a) members are trying hard enough, (b) work processes need improving, (c) more resources are needed, etc. Groups without these goals and benchmarks tend to be less successful.

Conclusion

Many leaders feel that they have little discretion in defining team goals because they are usually told what is required of the team. However, leaders always have considerable control over team or group goals. Directives from above are usually no more than vaguely defined intentions, e.g., integrate a new acquisition or figure out how to improve customer service. Leaders should use these directives as starting points for developing SMART-B and Vital Few goals for their groups and teams.

It is important that leaders work with their groups and teams to specify goals because clear goals enhance member understanding, commitment, cohesiveness and trust. It is also vital for virtual teams and groups to have a published set of SMART-B and Vital Few goals so that everything can be synchronized.

Finally, it is important for leaders to recognize how team goals influence group dynamics and performance. The goals of a group determine the nature of work to be performed, the number of people and skills required, the number of times members need to meet. the information that needs to be communicated, the budget and equipment required, and the strategies and tactics demanded to win.

Thus, team or group goals influence every other component of the Rocket Model. Leaders can improve team performance by setting goals that require interdependent effort and foster common fates; if, however, they only set individual goals, members will operate independently. Well-designed team and group goals combine leading and lagging indicators, adhere to the SMART criteria, and adopt internal and external performance benchmarks. Leaders need to create a set of Vital Few prioritized goals and use them to filter the impact of new events, to foster learning, to be proactive, to teach members how to win, and to celebrate success.

Mission Exercises and Activities

The Team Scorecard Exercise

Creating SMART-B and Vital Few group or team goals may appear easy, but it often takes considerable effort. Taking the time to do this right will pay huge dividends for leaders down the road as it will help everyone on the team to understand what the goals and benchmarks are, how they were created, and what tradeoffs and priorities were considered. Doing this activity helps team members understand what they need to do to improve commitment to goal accomplishment and to win. Given these benefits, the Team Scorecard Exercise has proven very helpful in the following situations:

- Launching new teams and groups.
- Creating goals for existing teams and groups that have no or ill-defined goals.
- Helping geographically dispersed members fully understand and buy in to the goals that need to be accomplished.
- Helping dysfunctional teams and groups determine some of the root causes of conflict.

Team Scorecard Exercise with teams and groups

Objective: The purpose of this exercise is for members to gain agreement and alignment around the team's key goals.

Room arrangement: A room that can hold everyone on the team, has additional space to do small group breakouts, and has enough wall space to post 10-18 flipcharts.

Time requirement: Usually 90-180 minutes.

Materials requirement: Flipchart paper, markers, masking tape, Team Scorecard example handouts and blank Team Scorecard forms for each member.

Leader Instructions:

1. Ask team members to review the team's assumptions and value proposition. Then ask them what goals the team needs to set to make the team value proposition become a reality. List their ideas on a flipchart. (It is highly recommended that teams and groups do the Context Assessment Exercise from Chapter 3 before creating their Team Scorecards.)

2. Review the SMART goal criteria, four performance benchmark levels, Team Scorecard example, and Team Scorecard form with the entire team.

3. If the team has more than six people, break into three or four person sub-groups. Divide the goal ideas among the sub-groups and ask them to create draft SMART-B goals and suggested review intervals (e.g., once a week, month, quarter, etc.) for each assigned idea. Sub-groups should create separate flipcharts for each SMART-B goal and appoint spokespersons.

4. Each sub-group should present its SMART-B goals and review intervals. The larger group discusses, debates, and modifies the goals, benchmarks, and review intervals as needed.

5. Once all of the goals have been presented and modified, explain the Vital Few concept and ask the team or group to identify its top one to three goals. This prioritizing can be done by either asking the team to come to consensus or by voting on the top goals. With the latter, members can be given three votes and asked to put checkmarks on the flipcharts containing the SMART-B goals that they feel are the most important. They should be able to distribute their votes any way they wish, so members could put all of their three votes on a single flipchart or single votes on three different flipcharts. Tally up the votes and come to consensus on the Vital Few goals and discuss their implications for the group.

6. Assign someone from the group to create an electronic copy of a completed Team Scorecard form. The scorecard should be sent out to all members for review and further comment.

7. Lastly, assemble all of the members to periodically review progress using the Team Scorecard. The scorecard should be a living document with goals and benchmarks added, modified and deleted over time.

The Rocket Model

Team Scorecard Form

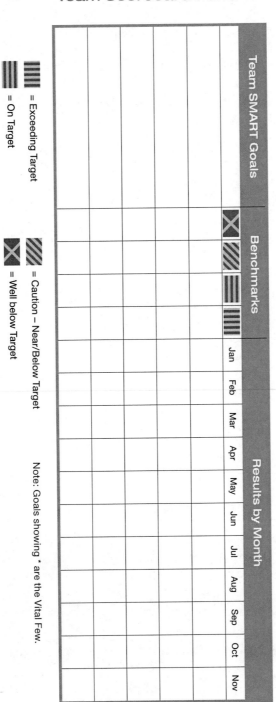

||| = Exceeding Target

||| = On Target

⊠ = Well below Target

▨ = Caution – Near/Below Target

Team SMART Goals	Benchmarks	Jan	Feb	Mar	Apr	May	Jun	Jul	Aug	Sep	Oct	Nov

Results by Month

Note: Goals showing * are the Vital Few.

[5]

Talent—Who Is on the Bus?

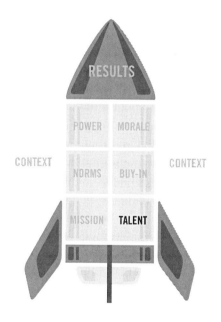

[**Talent Key Points**

1. Size matters.

2. Strategy drives structure and staffing.

3. Roles need to be clear.

4. Talent can be built or bought.

5. Followership types are important.

6. Team killers need team sheriffs.]

Sigma was a successful global airline with five major hubs across the United States and daily flights to over 500 cities. Sigma also operated ten gateways (slightly smaller facilities located in major cities with higher volumes of domestic traffic and a small number of international flights). One of Sigma's gateways on the West Coast averaged 25 domestic arrivals and departures per day and two direct flights to and from Asia and Europe. This gateway employed a station director, six direct reports on the management team, and approximately 150 ground staff. The gateway operated flights all day, seven days a week, with the staff working one of two shifts each day.

Three years ago, the gateway began experiencing problems; its on-time departure statistics dropped into the lowest quartile, and its lost baggage claims (particularly luggage transferred between code share partner airplanes) increased, eroding the company's reputation among business customers. Passenger complaints, employee grievances, and hotline calls increased; these problems, along with high levels of mechanic and baggage handler turnover, created havoc in gateway operations.

Steve Johnson had been appointed station director four years earlier; using retirements, transfers, and promotions, he assembled a management team composed of his personal favorites. Like many managers, Steve thought he was a good judge of talent, but his team resembled the cast from "The Island of Misfit Toys."

- Joanne, the assistant director, was a bossy know-it-all who constantly complained about Sigma airlines to anyone who would listen. She refused to talk to anyone she thought incompetent, which was almost everyone.

- Connie, who was in charge of half of the mechanics, ground crew, and baggage handlers, was a nice person who would yield to anyone who challenged her. She was also recovering from lung cancer and could no longer work full time.

- Mark, a bully, was in charge of the other half of the mechanics, ground crew, and baggage handlers. His military background prompted him to see his peers as adversaries and his staff as lowly privates. He was competitive, arrogant, and mean; referring to Connie, he told his staff that airline operations was no place for someone with one lung and suggested that she retire.

- Seth supervised the gate, ticket, and baggage claim agents; he was manipulative and mischievous and loved to hear gossip, spread rumors, spur reactions, and stay in the limelight.

- Sudhir, in control of similar staff, was a technical wizard who somehow gained access to Steve's e-mail and conference calls.

- Bill was a "Steady Eddie" who provided oversight for the various shifts during the week; he had been at the gateway for 30 years and learned the key to survival long ago: keep his head down, do his job, and do not become involved in office politics.

In time, Sigma's upper management noticed the gateway's terrible performance data. Once Steve came under the corporate microscope, he did what many do in these situations—he joined a competitor. This gave Sigma a double win—i.e., an incompetent manager joined a competitor—but it left a mess to be cleaned up. Robbie Jones was hired to turn the situation around. Originally joining Sigma as a baggage handler, Robbie moved through the ranks over a period of 20 years before becoming the station director at several small airports. Moving the gateway operations to a higher level would be the biggest challenge he had faced in his career.

Talent Defined

In his book *Good to Great*, Jim Collins notes that the first thing great companies must do is to get the right people on the bus.[38] One of a leader's key responsibilities is to get the right people on the team or group. However, like Robbie, many leaders must drive busses that are full of people who have a ticket to ride based on politics, simple availability, or favoritism instead of the knowledge or skills needed for team goal accomplishment. Leaders should never squander opportunities to choose their own players—it is a privilege few ever have.

The *Talent* component of the Rocket Model concerns the number, skills, and roles of people in a team or group. What a group or team is trying to accomplish (i.e., *Mission*) should determine the number and type of people needed. Getting this right is a challenge for any leader. For example, in 1939, President Franklin D. Roosevelt went through 50 candidates before selecting George Marshall to become Chief of Staff for the U. S. Army.[39] Peter Drucker noted that companies only have a .333 batting average for selecting successful executives;[40] moreover, many leaders choose candidates casually, leading to even worse batting averages.

A simple way for leaders to determine whether their teams have the right people is to answer the five *right* questions. Do their teams or groups

- Have the *right* number of people?
- With the *right* skills?
- In the *right* roles?
- At the *right* time?
- For the *right* reasons?

If the answer is "no" to any of these questions, the team may suffer from a talent problem. Although leaders rarely admit they are poor judges of talent, they may admit to having many B or C level players. On the one hand, these leaders may not have enough time to select team members efficiently; on the other hand, they are willing to waste resources trying to support their weakest players. Good leaders are efficient talent managers, regardless of whether they choose or inherit their players. If they inherit their players, then one of the first things they do is evaluate and upgrade team talent; less effective leaders choose poor players, have lax standards for talent, and are reluctant to pull the trigger on poor performers. Good leaders are always developing and recruiting new talent.

There are some standard questions leaders should ask about their team talent: some have clear answers; the answers to others are largely contextual. Leaders may be the only people who can answer certain questions; other questions may need group member input. Leaders need to find answers to team talent questions, and this chapter provides the procedure.

Key Talent Questions

1. How many people should be on the team?
2. What comes first: picking the team or setting team goals?
3. Should team member roles be vague or specific?
4. What if there is a shortfall of talent?
5. What role does followership play in team performance?
6. What should be done with team killers?

How Many People Should Be on a Team?

The key driver of team or group size is the team's scorecard. Figuring out what a team needs to succeed is more important than determining how many people are needed—the more members, the harder it is to build teams. Pair-wise relationships needed to do joint work increases exponentially with team membership.[41] Therefore, once there are more than 20-25 people, the group does better operating with sub-teams (or groups). For example, a National Football League team may call itself a team, but it will really operate as a group with different sub-teams (i.e., the offense, defense, and special teams units).

Leaders tend to have too many rather than too few people, and in either case, performance suffers. Many committees, community groups, executive teams, and task forces are simply too big to be effective. Although aggregating ideas from a wide range of people helps generate better solutions and creates buy-in, leaders usually need to create a sub-set of members to drive implementation. Leaders often make the mistake of including everyone during implementation and execution, an error which results in no accountability. Thus, team size may vary depending on whether the problem is to formulate or to implement solutions, and larger teams are not necessarily more effective than smaller teams.

As groups and teams increase in size, members have increasing difficulty identifying with one another. Hackman and his associates studied 120 executive teams and found that 90 percent disagreed about who was on the team.[42] We worked with the executive leadership team of 18 members from a *Fortune* 500 high-tech firm. Scheduling meetings was a logistical nightmare, and making decisions was a near impossibility. The meetings usually involved a series of talking head presentations by staff personnel. We increased efficiency by reducing the number of team members from 18 to 12 and by recommending that a sub-set of five executives meet more regularly to manage the business. Although this process bruised some egos (nobody likes to get voted off the island), the company ran more effectively as a result.

What Comes First: Picking the Team or Setting Team Goals?

A few years ago we worked with a chief strategy officer of a *Fortune* 500 firm who said, "Strategy drives structure which drives staffing." He continued, "Organizations that screw up this sequence are themselves likely to be screwed up. Letting an organizational chart drive strategy or staffing an organization and then figuring out what everyone is supposed to do are recipes for disaster." As obvious as this logic seems, many organizations fail to follow this sequence. Top leaders often surround themselves with sycophants who create strategies to justify their own empires. Family businesses are particularly prone to ignoring the sequence and suffer as a result.

The corollary is that team goals determine team size, team organization, and required team skills. Consequently, leaders should study the goals to be achieved and the work to be performed *before* picking team members or defining team structure. This sequence also implies that leaders who inherit existing groups and teams should review the goals and define the ideal structure and skills needed by different team members. They can then compare the ideal team structure and skills set with that already in place to determine what changes are needed to improve team functioning and performance.

Should Team Member Roles Be Vague or Specific?

Leaders often must decide whether to define team member roles or leave things loose to maximize flexibility. Flexibility is important, but there are three reasons why leaders are better off setting clear expectations for team members. First, most people want to know their responsibilities, and research shows that role ambiguity creates employee dissatisfaction.[43] Second, clarifying team member expectations reduces intra- and inter-role conflict, which also adds to employee dissatisfaction and team dysfunction.[44] And third, when team performance declines, members can say, "It wasn't my fault," or "That's not my job" when expectations are not defined. It is easier to hold people accountable for performance or develop needed skills when role expectations are specified. Again, leaders need to make the implicit explicit by ensuring that their people know their roles and responsibilities.

What If There Is a Shortfall of Talent?

If leaders compare ideal structures and staffing models with the people they inherited, they usually find talent shortfalls. Turnover, changes in context and goals, the emergence of new processes and systems, and transitions from solution generation to implementation can also create gaps in talent. In such situations, leaders can either buy or build talent. Whether it is better to hire new people or develop the current team members depends on a number of factors: the magnitude of the shortfall, the urgency of goals, the available budget, the ramp up time, and the impact on team cohesiveness. Leaders should be aware of the importance of member stability on team performance. Teams whose members have worked together for long periods of time tend to perform at higher levels than those with high turnover.[45] It takes time for experienced team members to come up to speed with their new teams. (An experienced quarterback joining a new NFL team is a good example.) If sustained, superior performance is important, then leaders should focus more on developing internal talent than recruiting and on-boarding new team members.

What Role Does Followership Play in Team Performance?

Although a group or team may have SMART-B goals, a structure aligned with the goals, members with clearly defined roles, and all of the skills necessary to succeed, it may still have talent problems. One common problem involves what we call followership.[46, 47] Followership concerns the attitudes and behaviors that people demonstrate when in follower roles. More specifically, followership concerns the level of engagement and critical thinking skills demonstrated by team and group members. A group member may have all the right skills, yet sit in the corner and pout rather than perform. Other members may have fewer skills but work hard and offer good ideas for improving processes.

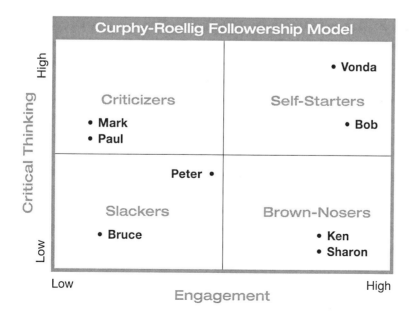

As seen in the diagram, engagement and critical thinking are independent dimensions of followership. These two dimensions can be divided into four followership types: Self-Starters, Brown-Nosers, Slackers, and Criticizers. The power of the model becomes obvious when leaders use it to assess the follower types on their team or group. Leaders need to manage the four types differently, so knowing members' types will provide leaders with insights on how to best manage the team.

Self-Starters, such as Bob and Vonda, are individuals who are passionate about working on the team and will try to make it successful. They also think of ways to improve team performance by raising issues, developing solutions, and showing enthusiasm. When they encounter problems, they resolve the issues by reporting what they have done rather than waiting to be told what to do. This follower type will improve their leader's performance by offering opinions before, and providing constructive feedback after, bad decisions.

Self-Starters are critical to the performance of teams and are the most effective follower type. A leader should keep in mind the psychological drivers of Self-Starters to best utilize their talents. Self-Starters are impatient and always thinking – in the shower, during a run, or over their Saturday morning coffee. They do not suffer fools gladly and expect their leaders to set goals, clarify roles, clear obstacles, and provide resources needed to succeed. A leader who dithers, plays favorites, makes bad decisions, or fails to follow through on commitments discourages Self-Starters. Self-Starters want to share their ideas promptly and want feedback even after work. If a leader wants to encourage Self-Starters, he or she needs to articulate a clear value proposition and to establish a defined set of goals for teams because Self-Starters prefer to seek forgiveness rather than permission. If Self-Starters do not know where the team is going and what the rules are, then they may take actions that are counterproductive. A word of warning: If Self-Starter's decisions are ignored, they are likely to become Criticizers or Slackers. A leader also needs to provide Self-Starters with necessary resources, interesting and challenging work, regular performance feedback, recognition for good performance, and promotion opportunities. The bottom line is that Self-Starters can be rewarding but challenging team members. A leader needs to be responsive and bring his or her A game to work to encourage these followers.

Brown-Nosers such as Ken and Sharon have a strong work ethic but lack critical thinking skills. Brown-Nosers rarely point out problems, raise objections, or make waves because they are dutiful, conscientious, and accommodating. Brown-Nosers constantly check with their leader and operate by seeking permission rather than forgiveness. Flattering Brown-Nosers often surround an egocentric, autocratic leader. Brown-Nosers usually go far in organizations, particularly in those that lack objective performance metrics. Organizations lacking clear measures of performance often make personnel decisions based on politics, and Brown-Nosers play politics very well.

Because Brown-Nosers are unwilling to raise objections, teams and organizations consisting of Brown-Nosers make bad decisions and depend entirely on their leaders to be successful. Leaders can do several things to convert Brown-Nosers into Self-Starters, but the first step is to understand that Brown-Nosers are primarily driven by fear of failure. Brown-Nosers often have all the experience and technical expertise needed to resolve issues but lack the self-confidence needed to make decisions because they do not want to make senseless mistakes. Therefore, to convert Brown-Nosers, a leader needs to focus on boosting their self-confidence. Whenever Brown-Nosers describe problems, the leader needs to ask how they think these problems should be resolved; putting the burden of resolving the problem on them will enhance their critical thinking skills and self-confidence. If possible, a leader should support the solutions offered, provide reassurance, resist interfering when solutions are not working, and periodically ask the Brown-Nosers what they have learned by implementing their own solutions. Brown-Nosers should only be rewarded for providing positive results – it is damaging when others in the organization think their sycophantic behavior is rewarded. Brown-Nosers have made the transition to Self-Starters when they openly challenge the leader and provide alternative solutions.

Bruce and Peter are Slackers; they don't work very hard, think they deserve a paycheck for just showing up, and believe it is the leader's job to solve problems. Slackers are clever at avoiding work, often disappear for hours, look busy but get little done, have good excuses for not completing projects, and spend more effort finding ways to avoid finishing tasks than they would by just doing them. Slackers are stealth employees who are happy to spend their time surfing the Internet, shopping online, gossiping with co-workers, and taking breaks with no concern for their jobs. Nonetheless, Slackers want to stay off their boss' radar screens, so they often do just enough to stay out of trouble but never more than their peers.

Turning Slackers into Self-Starters is challenging because a leader needs to enhance both their engagement and critical thinking skills. Many believe Slackers lack motivation. They have motivation; however, it's directed towards matters unrelated to work. They work hard playing videogames, riding motorcycles, fishing, or operating side businesses. Asking them about their hobbies will cause their passion to become evident. Slackers work to live, rather than living to work, and they view work as a way to support their preferred pursuits. Thus, the psychological driver for Slackers is motivation for work; leaders need to persuade these individuals to focus more energy on their job activities. One way to do this is to assign them tasks more in line with their hobbies. For example, give followers who enjoy surfing the Internet, research projects to improve their motivation. Improving job fit is another way to improve work motivation; if followers are assigned positions within teams or organizations that fit their interests, their engagement and critical thinking skills may also improve.

A leader who wants to convert Slackers into Self-Starters also needs to consider whether his or her own performance is contributing to followers' disengagement and uncritical thinking levels. Slackers may be Self-Starters who lack the necessary equipment, technology, or funding and have given up. In other cases, a leader may be aloof, playing games or favorites, or unable to make decisions, thereby causing others to stop making meaningful contributions. If followers have the resources they need and favoritism is not an issue, then a leader needs to set objectives, provide feedback about work performance, and gradually increase performance standards. Slackers prefer to remain anonymous; telling them that they can either perform at a higher level or becoming the focus of their leader's attention may improve their work motivation and productivity. Nonetheless, converting Slackers to Self-Starters is a difficult and time-consuming endeavor and may not be possible. Thus, a leader may find it easier to replace Slackers with potential Self-Starters than spend time on these conversion efforts.

Finally, *Criticizers* are followers with strong thinking skills who are disengaged. Rather than directing their analytical skills to productive outcomes, they find fault in anything their leaders and organizations do. Criticizers educate co-workers about their leaders' shortcomings, how change efforts will fail, how poorly their organization compares to the competition, and how management ignores their suggestions. They constantly complain about current or past grievances. In terms of their impact on team and organizational performance, they are the most dangerous of the four types because their personal mission is to create dissent. They are often the first to greet new employees in order to tell them "how things really work around here." Because misery loves company, they tend to hang out with other Criticizers. If not managed properly, Criticizers can take over teams and entire departments. Dealing with them can be the most difficult challenge a leader faces.

Most Criticizers were once Self-Starters who became disenchanted because they identified (with their strong critical thinking skills) problems in their leader's performance. In addition, Criticizers are offended when a leader rewards Brown-Nosers in the absence of any significant performance. A leader can also create Criticizers by being arrogant, micromanaging work, or failing to listen to the staff. Because Criticizers are motivated to create converts, they resemble an organizational cancer; like many cancers, they respond best to aggressive treatment. A leader needs to understand that Criticizers are acutely sensitive to any breach of trust. They act out because they crave recognition and are angry about not receiving any. As noted, some Criticizers were Self-Starters who satisfied their recognition needs through their work accomplishments but were somehow not recognized or promoted when they felt they deserved it, lost prestige and authority for unfair reasons, or worked for a boss who was threatened by their problem-solving skills. Leaders will have no chance converting these people until they are able to align their actions with the values they expect from the organization. If the alignment happens, leaders can begin reconverting Criticizers to Self-Starters by finding opportunities to recognize them publicly.

Criticizers are good at pointing out the fallacies in decisions and change initiatives. When they raise objections, a leader needs to thank them for their input and ask how they think the issues should be resolved. Criticizers may initially resist offering solutions because their previous suggestions have been ignored, but a leader needs to break through this resistance and press Criticizers for help. Once Criticizers offer solutions that a leader can live with, these solutions need to be adopted, and Criticizers need to be publicly thanked for their input. Repeating this pattern of soliciting solutions, adopting suggestions, and publicly recognizing Criticizers for their efforts helps convert them into Self-Starters. If a leader repeatedly attempts to engage Criticizers and they fail to respond, then termination becomes a viable option. However, when a Criticizer is terminated, the leader should look in the mirror and ask what he or she did to lose the confidence of these good thinkers. Nonetheless, if Criticizers are not dealt with aggressively, a leader may end up leading teams composed only of Criticizers.

Several aspects of the followership model require additional comment. First, leaders can use the model to understand group dynamics and what is needed to improve team talent within any team or group. Second, these four follower types can and do change over time. Members who were once Self-Starters can become Criticizers and vice-versa. Leaders usually determine whether members become Brown-Nosers, Slackers, Criticizers, or Self-Starters.[48] Because follower types are dynamic, leaders should periodically assess their own behavior and use the followership model to evaluate the impact it has on the people in their groups. Third, leaders need to realize that their own follower types affect the teams and groups they lead.[49] For example, the story about the airline gateway at the beginning of this chapter described Joanne and Mark, who were Criticizers. What would it be like to work for these people, and how would their behavior affect the follower types of the people they lead? Obviously, teams and groups with higher percentages of Self-Starters are more likely to be successful than those composed of Criticizers and Slackers.[50]

What Do You Do with Team Killers?

Team Killers are proficient individuals who, for some reason, do not play well with others.[51] An example might be a skilled software engineer on a product development team who thinks that the team is lucky to have him and that his peers are incompetent. Team Killers' arrogance, unwillingness to help others, and selfish attitudes have corrosive effects on group dynamics.

A leader is often unsure about how to handle Team Killers. Although Team Killers often have skills that are critical to group and team success, their attitudes disrupt the rest of the team. Team Killers are essentially Criticizers—they are usually angry about some perceived slight, and they crave attention, usually at another's expense. Consequently, a leader can deal with Team Killers in one of two ways. The leader can be positive and solicit Team Killers for advice on how to solve team problems, implement the advice that make sense, and publicly recognize them for their ideas. However, the conversion of Team Killers into Self-Starters may not be possible because of the difficulty in meeting their every expectation. Another option is for the leader to play sheriff by setting clear expectations and holding Team Killers accountable for their disruptive behavior. This approach is the one most commonly taken, but the leader will need to find alternatives for the knowledge provided by the Team Killers because they are more likely to leave than change their behavior.

Conclusion

History shows that the laboratories with the best researchers, the flying units with the best pilots, and the teams with the best athletes usually win, and it is a leader's responsibility to recruit the best people. Although talent is a key determinant of team and group effectiveness, leaders rarely obsess over talent. Those who do constantly assess, develop, and upgrade their staffs are often seen as talent magnets—many of the best employees want to work on these teams to enhance their skills. Unfortunately, leaders do not pay enough attention to upgrading talent. They tend to make quick but flawed decisions about people and then live with what they have rather than replacing the weak members or developing their Bs into A players.

This chapter reviewed six key talent questions leaders need to answer to improve group effectiveness and build high-performing teams. These questions concern determining the right number of people for the team or group, identifying team goals to drive structure and staffing decisions, clarifying team member roles, finding the trade-offs between building and buying talent, understanding how followership affects team dynamics, and deciding what to do about team killers. Our experience is that few leaders recognize these questions or know how to answer them. This, of course, is worrisome because leaders are responsible for staffing their groups or teams. The caliber of talent found on a group or team directly impacts a leader's effectiveness. Leaders who tolerate B and C players and surround themselves with Brown-Nosers, Slackers, and Criticizers are also B or C players. Unfortunately B and C level leaders outnumber the A players. This chapter can help B and C leaders move up a level by improving the talent on their groups and teams.

There is one final caution about team talent. The information about the four types of followers suggests that leaders can afford to be careless only when they are dealing with Brown-Nosers. Not true—Careless leader behavior around the other three types leads to disaffection, alienation, and poor performance.

Talent Exercises and Activities

Roles and Responsibility Matrices

Although there are many different activities leaders can use to assess and develop team talent, we are going to review the Roles and Responsibility Matrix and Followership Scatterplot. The Roles and Responsibility Matrix can be useful in the following situations:

- Helping new and existing teams and groups define the roles to be played by each member.

- Helping geographically dispersed members fully understand the roles and responsibilities of all members.

- Helping dysfunctional teams and groups determine some of the root causes of conflict.

Roles and Responsibility Matrix with teams and groups.

Objective: The purpose of the Roles and Responsibility Matrix is to clarify responsibilities and expectations for individual team members.

Room arrangement: Ideally a room with ample space to hold everyone on the team and to post several flipcharts around the walls.

Time requirement: About 60 minutes.

Materials requirement: Flipchart paper, markers, masking tape, Roles and Responsibility Matrix example handouts and blank Roles and Responsibility Matrix forms for each member.

Leader Instructions:

1. Explain the purpose. Review the Roles and Responsibility Matrix example so team members understand the end product.

2. Review the team's goals and then ask the team to name the critical tasks and activities that must be performed to achieve the goals. Write the tasks on a flipchart.

3. Tape several flipcharts to the right and then draw lines to create a blank Roles and Responsibility Matrix next to the flipchart. Write team member names across the top of the Roles and Responsibility Matrix on the appropriate flipcharts.

4. Taking one critical task at a time, ask the group to identify the one team member who has primary responsibility (P) for task success. Identification can be done by having team members volunteer, having a discussion and coming to consensus, or getting everyone to vote on the assignment of primary responsibility. Write a P in the appropriate box on the Responsibility Matrix.

5. Once the P is assigned, determine if any team members have secondary responsibilities (S) for the task or activity. This can be done the same way the Ps were assigned and write Ss in the appropriate boxes on the Responsibility Matrix. Repeat this process until all the critical tasks have one P and all needed Ss assigned.

6. Once all the Ps and Ss have been assigned, review the responsibilities for each team member. Do some team members have significantly more or less work than others? If so, then the team may need to reassign some responsibilities to balance workloads. In addition, the team should determine if it has any skill gaps and then create plans to build or buy needed talent.

7. Assign someone from the group to make an electronic copy of the final Roles and Responsibility Matrix to send out for review to all the members.

Roles and Responsibilities Matrix Example

Team Name: Bank Senior Leadership Team

Team Goals: a) Pass FDIC examinations
b) Launch dealer banking programs
c) Expand credit card offerings

Critical Tasks/ Responsibilities (P) or (S)	Team Members							
	Ray	Craig	Mike	Debbie	Charlene	Steve	Chuck	Cheryl
Market research on credit card opportunities					P		S	
Preparation of credit card marketing campaign					P		S	
Launch direct mail for credit cards			P				S	
Create risk protocols		S				P		
Conduct credit card invoice quality checks		P					S	
Identify dealer banking in MN, TX, and CO	S			P				S

P = Primary Responsibility
S = Secondary Responsibility

Roles and Responsibilities Matrix

Team Name: _____

Team Goals: a) _____

b) _____

c) _____

Critical Tasks/ Responsibilities (P) or (S)	Team Members							

P = Primary Responsibility
S = Secondary Responsibility

Followership Scatterplots

Since they can be quite disruptive if done in team settings, Followership Scatterplots are usually only done by leaders. This exercise has proven useful in the following situations:

- Helping leaders gain insight into the types of followers on their teams.
- Helping leaders gain insight into the underlying drivers of member behavior and dysfunctional group dynamics.
- Providing leaders with ideas on how to manage different members.

Followership Scatterplot

Room arrangement: A room that provides a high degree of privacy.

Time requirement: 30-60 minutes.

Materials requirement: Blank Followership Scatterplot form.

Leader Instructions:

1. Pick a team member.

2. Read the Critical Thinking descriptions at the left of the Followership Scatterplot and give the team member a Critical Thinking score.

3. Read the Engagement descriptions at the bottom of the Followership Scatterplot and give the team member an Engagement score.

4. Write the team member's name or initials at the intersection of the two scores.

5. Repeat steps 1-4 for the remaining members of the team.

6. Draw your folllowership history. Begin by placing a dot on the Followership Scatterplot that represents the followership type you exhibited at your first job, then draw a line to depict how your followership type changed over the course of your career.

7. Identify the main reasons why your followership type changed over time. If you are like most people, your immediate supervisor had a profound impact on your followership type. Think about this pattern as you review the followership types of your direct reports.

8. Use the Followership Scatterplot results to identify the biggest opportunities to improve talent. What could you as a leader do differently to improve the followership types of your staff? Would the team or group benefit most by converting one or two Brown-Nosers or Criticizers into Self-Starters or by replacing a Slacker? Identify one or two personal leadership behaviors and one or two team members that you want to change and use the Followership Action Plan to document the steps needed to make this happen.

Followership Action Plan

Who	What they need to work on	How you will help them

Creative, innovative, independent minded thinker. Challenges the status quo and constantly looks for ways to improve the organization. Has a strong dislike for being told what to do and how to do things.

At times, will develop new ideas for improvement. Will challenge orders, directives and policies if they do not seem to make sense. Like to make decisions for themselves.

Takes direction, usually will not challenge decisions. Needs to be asked before offering suggestions for improvement.

Prefers structured, unambiguous work settings with roles and polices governing work behaviors. Will only challenge authority if decisions are extremely important to them.

Follows rules, procedures, directives and orders blindly. Never challenges authority. Wants to be specifically told what to do and how to do things. Extremely dislikes making decisions. Wants lots of reassurance before they make a decision. Likes structure.

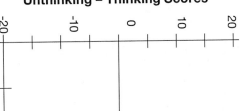

Unthinking – Thinking Scores

20 10 0 -10 -20

Disengagement – Engagement Scores

-20 -10 0 10 20

Needs constant prodding and close supervision before tasks are completed. Does the absolute minimum necessary to get by. Gets little done.

Most efforts come up a bit short in quality, efforts can wax and wane. Can usually be counted on the get the job done, but timeliness or quality can suffer at times.

Overall a solid performer, but Puts in extra hours when necessary, produces higher than average work than peers. Usually will take ownership for results.

Above average performer. Puts in extra hours in long hours, persists on tasks until complete. Actively looks for ways to contribute to organizational success. Takes ownership for and pride in results.

Readily goes the extra mile. Puts in long hours, persists on tasks until complete. Actively looks for ways to contribute to organizational success. Takes ownership for and pride in results.

[6]

Norms—What Are the Rules?

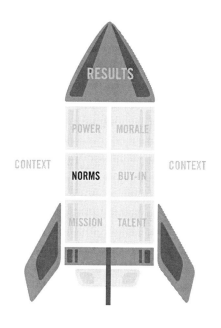

Norms Key Points

1. Norms are unwritten rules.

2. Norms pertain to how things get done.

3. Norms get stronger over time.

4. Leaders fail to take advantage of norms.

5. Norms need to be aligned with goals.

6. Four norms are critical to team success.

Dave was the new CEO of a high tech *Fortune* 1000 company that designed components for PCs, servers, tablets, video-game consoles, and mobile phones. Dave had advanced quickly through the ranks and managed the company's engineering function before becoming the CEO. Dave was a typical hardware engineer—introverted, organized, results-oriented, and extremely bright.

Like many new CEOs, Dave wanted to be inclusive, so he created an executive team with 18 senior leaders. Half were long-term employees retained from the previous CEO; the others were people Dave hired to help drive the company's strategic plan.

Over the past five years the company had grown through acquisition. One major acquisition built components that provided different but complementary functionality to the organization's current product line. The company's strategic plan was to create integrated components that combined the best features from both companies. If the organization could overcome the engineering challenges associated with the acquisition's different technology, then it would leapfrog its competition and realize dramatic increases in market share, revenues, and margins.

The executive team met every two months to review financial statements, operating statistics, marketing initiatives, sales, and strategic plans. These two-day meetings took place in the company board room that only had 12 chairs around the table, so some had to sit along the walls at the back of the room. The meetings were tightly scripted and generally consisted of staffers delivering a series of 30- to 60-minute, detailed PowerPoint presentations with little time for questions or discussion.

During these meetings, Dave sat in a chair at the front of the board room and focused on the speakers. The rest of the executive team spent the meeting on their laptops, iPads, or Blackberrys, dealing with other matters. They had little to say when it was time to ask questions or discuss issues. As a result Dave asked most of the questions and made most of the decisions in the meetings.

With Dave's unilateral decision-making, his apathetic team avoided controversial topics. Dave wanted to use the bi-monthly meetings to transform his direct reports into a high-performing team; however, he soon realized that the meetings were having the opposite effect. He realized that he had to fix this problem quickly, or he would lose any chance of his direct reports being able to operate as a cohesive team.

Norms Defined

Norms are unwritten rules that guide human behavior, e.g., elevator and airport security line etiquette. Most people know what to do when entering an elevator full of strangers: enter the elevator, face the door, don't make eye contact or engage in conversation, and leave quickly when reaching the desired floor. In airport security lines: take a bin; quickly fill it with shoes, jackets, laptops, liquids, etc.; put the bin and any luggage on the conveyor belt; walk through the body scanner; and then, like Lucille Ball in the candy factory, reassemble everything as quickly as possible. Like all norms, those governing elevator and security line behavior are not written down, but everyone is expected to abide by them. People who don't observe the norms are considered aberrant.

How do Norms relate to the other elements in building executive teams? Context describes *what* situations face the team; Mission, *what* the team is to accomplish; Talent, *what* roles team members play; and Norms, *how* the team gets things done. Norms develop as soon as a group of people are assembled.[52] Within an hour or so of first meeting, groups will develop rules for greeting, communicating, and making decisions. The longer a group has been together, the more entrenched its norms become. Some groups even develop their own language in the form of TLAs (three-letter acronyms). Seating arrangements, pecking orders, meeting schedules and behaviors, dress codes, presentation formats and styles, decision-making processes, work hand-offs, and performance standards are all common team norms. Norms are typically obvious to outsiders but often invisible to insiders. Unfortunately, a team's rules of the road are usually implicit, leading newbies to annoy more seasoned team members by wearing the wrong clothes, sitting in the wrong seats, or raising forbidden topics.

Key Norm Questions

1. Are the team's norms helping or hindering team performance?

2. Which norms are the most important?

3. Does the team have the right operating rhythm?

4. How should team members communicate with each other?

5. How should the team make decisions?

6. Are there any consequences for norm violations or sub-standard performance?

Although they are implicit, norms potently affect team member behavior and represent a powerful lever that leaders can use to change team and group dynamics. Surprisingly, we find that Norms are often one of the lowest scoring components in the Rocket Model, and many leaders are either oblivious to the norms that are in effect or unaware of how to change them. In contrast, effective leaders imbed the right norms into their groups and teams. This chapter shows how to utilize norms to their best advantage.

Are the Team's Norms Helping or Hindering Team Performance?

Leaders first need to decide whether the norms currently in place help or hinder team performance. It might seem obvious that a team's rules would enhance cohesiveness and performance, but the story at the beginning of this chapter shows how they can do the opposite. Leaders can do several things to ensure that norms contribute to team performance. First, they need to assess the current norms, a challenging task because norms are so incorporated in day-to-day activities that they can be difficult to identify. One way to make implicit norms explicit is to ask the team members to discuss the rules regarding team meetings, communication and decision-making processes, and other key aspects of group functioning.
Team members need to come to a consensus as to when the team meets, who attends, what is discussed, how decisions are made, whether it is okay to show up late or leave early, etc. Leaders and members should then review the team's goals and discuss whether the current norms help or hinder team functioning. If some of these informal rules impede success, leaders and members should devise new norms and ensure that they are implemented.

Which Norms Are the Most Important?

Although teams have many norms, some are more important than others. For example, operating rhythm, communication, decision-making and accountability norms have the biggest impact on cohesiveness and performance.[53, 54] A team's operating rhythm concerns how meetings are run. Unfortunately, many leaders do not know how to run efficient team meetings. If team members complain about being kept in the dark, their confidential conversations being divulged or difficult topics being circumvented, communication may be a problem. If leaders make autocratic decisions, or conversely, if groups make too many decision by consensus, decision-making may be a problem. If leaders play favorites or fail to hold members accountable for their performance or misbehavior, team morale and performance may be a problem.

Does the Team Have the Right Operating Rhythm?

Patrick Lencioni once said that a meeting should be like a good movie in that it should keep people engaged.[55] If so, then most business meetings would merit The Razzies or Rotten Tomatoes award because they are so dull. Meetings are crucial for reviewing progress, solving problems, celebrating successes, changing norms, and boosting morale. Sorting out some simple meeting mechanics—meeting frequency, the purpose and length of the meetings, the discussion focus, and the attendees—can help improve team functioning. Leaders should work with their groups to develop rules for expected behavior during meetings so that members are less concerned about their mobile devices and more focused on the meeting's agenda. Furthermore, the power of a team's operating rhythm should not be underestimated. A senior leader, upon becoming a CEO, changed the executive leadership team's operating rhythm to send a message about what he would pay attention to and how he expected others to behave. Unfortunately, this technique is not as common as one might wish. Most leaders make a big mistake by letting norms evolve independently rather than leveraging those norms advantageously.

How Should Team Members Communicate with each Other?

We have seen breakdowns in communication cause many organizational problems in groups and teams. What, how, and when information is communicated, the level of confidentiality, inquiry response times, and permission to raise controversial topics are some implicit communication norms that wreck many teams. The higher a team is in an organization, the more energy the participants spend reducing conflict through self-censorship.[56] We worked with a leadership team that stated publicly that all was well but admitted privately that they came to meetings with their lips stapled. Although several controversial issues were ripping the team apart, no one broached the topics for fear of destroying team morale. We explained that the issues were already having a negative effect, and, to reduce the negativity, they needed publicly to address the issues. It is important to encourage teams to address controversial topics correctly because failing to do so only further damages cohesiveness and effectiveness.

How Should the Team Make Decisions?

President Lyndon Johnson once said, "There are two kinds of animals in the White House—elephants and ants. And I am the only elephant."[57] President Johnson's rules for decision-making were crystal clear, but most groups and teams have vague or sub-optimal decision-making rules. Many members have more problems with their teams' decision-making processes than with the actual decisions. For example, members become frustrated when decisions made by the accountable member of the team are overruled by the leader. Frustration also occurs when teams suffer from analysis paralysis when making minor decisions or when they confuse debate with decision-making.

Teams generally make decisions in one of three ways, all with different consequences. *Autocratic* decisions work best when the person making the decisions has all the information and authority needed to make the call. This individual does not need to be the leader because members can make autocratic decisions within their scope of responsibilities. Although autocratic decisions are efficient—if members believe decision-makers lack credibility—execution, morale, and levels of buy-in will be affected.

Decision-Making Continuum

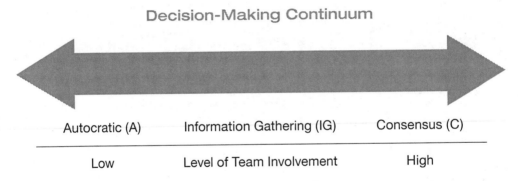

Autocratic (A)	Information Gathering (IG)	Consensus (C)
Low	Level of Team Involvement	High

The *Information-Gathering* approach is used when the individual with the authority lacks the information needed to make good decisions. People who use this method solicit others for information and recommendations but reserve the right to make final decisions. This decision-making process is more time consuming and can lead to false expectations among the members as they may believe that they are working towards a *Consensus* decision. A Consensus decision-making process involves teams working together to find mutually satisfying solutions. Despite being overused and taking the most time, this approach yields higher levels of innovation and ownership.

Common Group and Team Decision-Making Mistakes

1. Overuse of either the Autocratic or Consensus approaches.

2. Believing one style is being employed (i.e., Consensus) when another style is actually used (i.e., Information-Gathering)

3. Assuming there is agreement on problems and solutions when none exists. Because members often place harmony over accuracy, they are likely not to raise objections for fear of alienating others, causing teams to make decisions that none of the individual members agree with.[58]

4. Failure to make a decision on an issue. Many teams and groups suffer from analysis paralysis or a lack of intestinal fortitude. It is often better to make a decision and modify it as needed rather than let the issue languish.

5. Confusing debate with decision-making. Leaders and teams have not made decisions until there has been some observable change in behavior. If there is no discernible change, then there has been no real decision.

Teams make five common mistakes teams regarding decision-making norms, and each is related to the three decision-making processes. Perhaps the most common mistake is a failure to make decisions. Oddly, teams often have long debates that result in no resolution. Teams may feel that they are producing change through these debates, but in reality they are just restating their intentions.

Are There Any Consequences for Norm Violations or Sub-Standard Performance?

The quote, "All animals are created equal, but some animals are more equal than others,"[59] applies to teams because few things can wreck team morale more quickly than favoritism. When members detect foul play, they can be expected to spend time complaining about the situations rather than doing what is needed for their teams to succeed. A related but even more prevalent problem for groups and teams is a lack of consequences. Too many leaders are more concerned about winning popularity contests than accomplishing team goals; consequently, they are reluctant to hold members accountable for sub-standard performance and norm violations. Leaders who play favorites or fail to maintain standards will eventually have teams full of Brown-Nosers, Slackers, and Criticizers.

Given the issues surrounding sub-standard performance and norm violations, every group and team needs a sheriff. Although members can play the role of team disciplinarian (e.g., shop stewards, athletic team captains, non-commissioned officers, etc.), more often than not the leaders must play this role. Leaders who set clear expectations, hold members accountable, and treat people fairly usually attract and/or retain Self-Starters even if there are Brown-Nosers, Slackers and Criticizers on the team. If leaders are unwilling to uphold standards and hold people accountable for their performance, they will create dysfunctional teams that won't achieve their goals.

Conclusion

Norms are at the core of teamwork because they regulate how things get done in groups or teams: when members meet, what happens in meetings, what issues can or cannot be raised, who makes the decisions, what information gets shared outside the group, and whether members are held accountable for their actions. Norms are powerful determinants of member behavior, team cohesiveness, and team performance, yet many leaders create problems by failing to realize the role that norms play in team dynamics. Leaders can choose the right people for their teams and help members understand the team's context and goals, but if they play favorites, run lousy meetings, make all the decisions, and have members who leak confidential information, then they will lead ineffective teams.

It is crucial that the executive leadership team have the right norms in place. The rest of the organization takes its cues from the top; therefore, if the top team has lousy meeting discipline, ineffective communication and decision-making processes, or there are perceptions of favoritism and poor accountability, then the rest of the organization follows suit. Executive leadership team dynamics are a key contributor to organizational performance, and their norms are often the cause of executive team dysfunction. The CEO's impact on executive leadership team norms filters down through the entire organizational culture. Therefore, the CEO is responsible for ensuring that executive leadership team norms and organizational culture are aligned with the company's strategy and key goals.

Norms Exercises and Activities

Setting Operating Rhythm Norms

The remainder of this chapter describes four exercises leaders can use with members to clarify, align, and set team norms. The operating rhythm exercise is concerned with setting meeting norms and is very useful in the following situations:

- Helping new teams and groups define the mechanics, rules of engagement, and structure of meetings.

- Helping existing teams revamp the mechanics, rules of engagement, and structure of meetings.

- Helping new or geographically dispersed members fully understand the mechanics, rules of engagement, and structure of meetings.

- Helping teams and groups determine some of the root causes of dysfunction and conflict.

Setting operating rhythm norms involves determining the (a) meeting mechanics (when, where, who, how long, etc.), (b) rules of engagement (punctuality, preparedness, use of laptops, etc.), and (c) meeting structure (goals, roles, agenda, and meeting improvements).

Objective: To create an agreed-upon set of mechanics, rules of engagement, and structures for teams and groups.

Room arrangement: Ideally a room with ample room to hold everyone on the team and enough wall space to post several flipcharts.

Time requirement: 60-90 minutes.

Materials requirement: Flipchart paper; markers; masking tape; Meeting Mechanics; Goals, Roles, Process, and Improvement (GRPI); and Rules of Engagement forms for each member.

Leader Instructions:

1. Explain that a team's operating rhythm concerns the mechanics, expected behaviors, and structure of team meetings.

2. Review the team's value proposition and goals with members. Emphasize how the operating rhythm needs to be aligned with what the team is trying to accomplish.

3. Review the Meeting Mechanics form and work with members to determine the purpose, dates, times, location, participants, etc. for each type of team meeting. Along these lines, it is recommended that many teams have more frequent but shorter "touch base" type meetings and less frequent (monthly or quarterly) meetings where they review scorecards, solve problems, create strategic plans, set budgets, etc. It is not uncommon for these two meetings to have different attendees.

4. If the group consists of more than eight members, then leaders may want to divide members into four- to six-person sub-groups and task them with creating the ideal Meeting Mechanics for the team. Have the sub-groups flipchart their proposed Meeting Mechanics and appoint spokespersons.

5. After each sub-group presents its results, the larger group discusses, debates, and agrees upon the final team Meeting Mechanics.

6. Leaders then review the Rules of Engagement form and work with the large group to set the behavioral expectations for all team meetings. The final set of expectations should be written on a flipchart.

7. Leaders should review the Goals, Roles, Process, and Improvement (GRPI) form and discuss how it can be used to structure team meetings. Work with the group to complete a GRPI form for the next team meeting. State that completed GRPI forms should be distributed to participants prior to all meetings. Work with the team to determine who is responsible for completing the forms and when they are to be distributed.

8. Assign someone from the group to make an electronic copy of the final Meeting Mechanics, Rules of Engagement, and completed GRPI forms and send it out to be reviewed by all team members.

9. Review the Meeting Mechanics, Rules of Engagement, and GRPI forms with the team on at least a quarterly basis to ensure meeting norms remain aligned with team goals.

Meeting Mechanics

Meeting Characteristics	Team Responses
Meeting Type/Purpose (Updates, Scorecard Reviews, Strategy Formulation, Budget Reviews, etc.)	
Dates (When should the meetings take place?)	
Length (How long will the meeting be?)	
Location (Where will the meetings take place?)	
Participants (Who attends?)	
Goals and Agendas (Who sets the meeting goals and agenda? How are topics added and when is the agenda sent?	

Rules of Engagement (ROE) Form

Suggested Rules	Team Responses
Punctuality/Attendance (Okay to show up late/ leave early/ skip meetings?)	
Meeting Management (Stick to agendas/okay to run late?)	
Do pre-work to prepare for meetings? (Yes/No? How much lead time?)	
Meeting Behavior (Openness, engagement, respect, equal participation, etc.)	
Use laptops, Blackberries, etc. (Okay or not okay? Or when is it okay?)	
Take calls during meetings? (Okay or not okay? Or when is it okay?)	
Send proxies or bring guests? (Okay or not okay? Or when is it okay?)	
Presentation Protocol (Bring hard copies of slides? Okay to ask questions during presentations or wait until the end?)	
Other ROEs	
Other ROEs	

Goals, Roles, Process and Improvement (GRPI) Form

Meeting Goals:

1.

2.

3.

4.

Meeting Roles:

- Who will create and send out the GRPI document:
- Who will send out meeting pre-work:
- Who will be the meeting facilitator/timekeeper:

Meeting Process:

- All participants sent meeting time, location, and GRPI?
- Meeting room reserved?
- Meeting audiovisual/telecommunication arrangements made?
- Meeting agenda:
  - GRPI overview (time)
  - Review of last meeting deliverables (time)
  - Key topics (list topics, presenters/leads, and time)
  - Review meeting next steps/deliverables/key messages (time)
  - Meeting improvements (time)

Meeting Improvements (At the end of the meeting, ask each participant):

- What worked in the meeting?
- What can be done to improve the meeting?

Setting Communication Norms

The Communication Norms checklist can be used to diagnose team communication processes and serve as a springboard to create new communications norms. The checklist can be useful in the following situations:

- Helping new teams establish communication norms.
- Helping geographically dispersed members identify potential communication breakdowns.
- Helping on-board new team members.
- Helping existing teams improve communication processes.
- Helping teams and groups determine some of the root causes of and develop solutions for dysfunction and conflict.

Setting communication norms involves working with members to assess current communication processes, identify opportunities for improvement, and set new norms.

Objective: To create an agreed-upon set of communication norms for teams and groups.

Room arrangement: Ideally a room with ample room to hold everyone on the team and enough wall space to post several flipcharts.

Time requirement: 60 minutes.

Materials requirement: Flipchart paper, markers, masking tape, Communication Norms checklists for each member.

Leader Instructions:

1. Send everyone a Communication Norms checklist that is to be completed and sent to a designated member of the team. Ask this member to tabulate the Communication Norms checklist results for the team. The tabulated results should include the number of 1s, 2s, etc. and the average score for each question on the checklist.

2. Get the team together and review the tabulated results for each question on Communication Norms checklist. Start with the overall level of team communication and ask members for their reactions to the results. Was anyone surprised, delighted, disappointed, etc.?

3. Review the rest of the results with the team and discuss what needs to be done to improve team communication norms. Write any agreed upon solutions on a flipchart.

4. Leaders in charge of new teams can skip steps 1 and 2 and can instead use the questions on the Communication Norms checklist to help their teams set communications norms.

5. Assign someone from the group to make an electronic copy of the new team communication norms and send it out to be reviewed by all team members.

6. Repeat steps 1-3 at least once every six months to ensure communication norms remain aligned with team goals.

Communication Norms Checklist

How would you rate:	Rating Scale 1=Poor 3=So-So 5=Outstanding
The overall level of team communication?	
The quality, quantity, and timeliness of the information you receive?	
The effectiveness of the team's primary communication mode (be it e-mail, voice mail, face-to-face interactions, etc.)?	
The extent you trust team members not to share private conversations or confidential information?	
The responsiveness of team members to others' requests?	
The level of participation of all members in team meetings?	
The degree to which difficult topics are raised and successfully resolved in team meetings?	

Setting Decision-Making Norms

The Decision-Making form can be used to diagnose team decision-making processes and help create new decision-making norms. The exercise can be useful in the following situations:

- Helping new teams establish decision-making norms.

- Helping geographically dispersed members identify potential decision-making breakdowns.

- Helping on-board new team members.

- Helping existing teams improve decision-making processes.

- Helping teams and groups determine some of the root causes of and develop solutions for dysfunction and conflict.

Setting decision-making norms involves working with members to assess current decision-making processes, identify opportunities for improvement, and set new norms.

Objective: To create an agreed-upon set of decision-making norms for teams and groups.

Room arrangement: Ideally a room with ample space to hold everyone on the team and enough wall space to post several flipcharts.

Time requirement: 60-90 minutes.

Materials requirement: Flipchart paper, markers, masking tape, Decision-Making forms for each member.

Leader Instructions:

1. Review the three primary decision-making processes (Autocratic, Information Gathering, and Consensus) with the group.

2. Create flipcharts that have the three columns and captions of the Decision-Making form and work with the group to identify all the decisions made over the past two to four weeks. Leaders will want to write down somewhere between 10-20 decisions in the left columns of the flipcharts. *Do not complete columns two and three at this time.*

3. Pass out the Decision-Making forms and ask everyone to individually complete all three columns for the decisions listed on the flipcharts.

4. Once everyone has completed the form, go through each decision one at a time and come to a consensus on the decision-making process used and final decision makers. Write the final answers for each decision on the flipcharts.

5. Determine if any changes need to be made to the decision-making norms once all the decisions have been reviewed. Are some decision-making styles overused or underutilized? Are all the right people making the decisions? How do the decisions made stack up against the team's Roles and Responsibility Matrix? What could the team do to improve its decision-making processes? Write down any future changes to the team's decision-making norms on a separate flipchart.

6. Leaders in charge of new teams can modify steps 2-5 to include 10-20 decisions the group will need to make over the next two to four weeks. Ask members to review the Roles and Responsibility Matrix (Chapter 5) and write down what they think the decision-making process and who the final decision maker should be for each decision. Discuss the results and note the final decision-making processes and decision makers on the flipcharts.

7. Assign someone from the group to make an electronic copy of the new team decision-making norms and send it to be reviewed by all team members.

8. Repeat steps 1-5 at least once every six months to ensure decision-making norms remain aligned with team goals.

Decision Making Form

What Topics/ Decisions?	How Made? A = Autocratic IG = Information Gathering C = Consensus	Final Decision Maker(s)?

Setting Accountability Norms

The Accountability Norms checklist can be used to determine the extent to which favoritism and accountability exists in teams and groups. Because leaders play a key role in these matters, the feedback obtained from the checklist is often a direct reflection of the leader's style. Leaders need to understand that they may get some unflattering feedback, but the ensuing discussions may be exactly what is needed to get groups and teams performing at higher levels. Nonetheless, leaders need to walk into this exercise with their eyes wide open. *If leaders do not really want to hear about the team's accountability norm, then they should forgo this exercise, as raising the issue and doing nothing about it is worse than never asking the question.* If leaders want to proceed down this path, then the checklist can be useful in the following situations:

- Helping new teams establish accountability norms.
- Helping geographically dispersed members identify potential accountability breakdowns.
- Helping on-board new team members.
- Helping existing teams improve perceptions of fairness, equity, and accountability.
- Helping teams and groups determine some of the root causes of and develop solutions for dysfunction and conflict.

Because of the sensitive nature of this topic, leaders may want someone from outside of the team to help facilitate this session. Setting accountability norms involves working with members to assess current perceptions of fairness, equity, and justice; identify opportunities for improvement; and set new norms.

Objective: To create an agreed-upon set of accountability norms for teams and groups.

Room arrangement: Ideally a room with ample room to hold everyone on the team and enough wall space to post several flipcharts.

Time requirement: 60-90 minutes.

Materials requirement: Flipchart paper, markers, masking tape, Accountability Norms checklists for each member.

Leader Instructions:

1. Send everyone an Accountability Norm checklist to be completed and sent to an outside facilitator or designated member of the team. Ask this person to tabulate the Accountability Norm checklist results for the team. The tabulated results should include the number of 1s, 2s, etc. and the average score for each question on the checklist.

2. Assemble the team and review the tabulated results for each question on Accountability Norms checklist. Start with the overall level of team accountability and ask members for their reactions to the results. Was anyone surprised, delighted, disappointed, etc.?

3. Review the rest of the results with the team and discuss what needs to be done to improve team accountability norms. Write any agreed-upon solutions on a flipchart.

4. Leaders in charge of new teams can skip steps 1 and 2 and use the questions on the Accountability Norms checklist to help their teams set communications norms.

5. Assign someone from the group to make an electronic copy of the new team accountability norms and send it to be reviewed by all team members.

6. Repeat steps 1-3 at least once every six months to ensure accountability norms remain aligned with team goals.

Accountability Norms Checklist

How would you rate:	Rating Scale 1=Poor 3=So-So 5=Outstanding
The clarity of team member roles?	
The clarity of assigned tasks and performance expectations?	
The clarity of team norms?	
The extent to which everyone on the team completes assigned tasks on time and with high quality?	
The extent to which team members take responsibility for their own mistakes?	
The extent to which team members are treated fairly and equitably?	
The extent to which all team members are held accountable for their behavior and performance?	

[7]

Buy-In—Are We All Committed to Win?

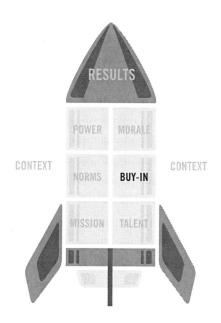

Bolen Technologies builds equipment that is widely used for supply chains. Over the last 30 years, the company had grown to generate over $1B in annual revenues. To remain the market leader, the company recently went through two major operational and cultural changes. The first involved off-shoring all equipment manufacturing to India and China to reduce costs. This change permitted significant cost reduction, but product quality and delivery times became problematic. The second major change included developing low-cost equipment to sell in the emerging South America, Africa, and Asian markets, but the process was taking too much time to design alternate products that were at suitable price points.

Randy Smith was in the telecommunications equipment business for 20 years before becoming CEO for Bolen Technologies in 2008. Randy, an analytical, strategic, and business-savvy executive, formulated the firm's new operational initiatives. Many of his direct reports doubted the initiatives, and their reservations filtered through the organization. This misalignment caused problems in quality, delivery, time to design, and price points.

Randy saw the emergence of new technology in his industry as an opportunity to double the business in five years. To help him grow Bolen, he hired a consultant named Connie as Director of Strategy. They spent a year analyzing all the information they could find and used it to formulate Bolen's new five-year vision, which contained five strategic initiatives. Those initiatives involved refining products, customer focus, and some geographic expansion. The company's new vision was sound, but it was so complicated that Randy needed 90 minutes to explain the vision to the Board of Directors and the executive leadership team. The board accepted Randy's vision, but his direct reports were skeptical of the company's ability to implement the changes.

Over the next six months, Randy's vision was rolled out to the next two layers of management, but they did not respond to the changes. Randy thought this disconnect was due to misgivings about the strategy and concerns over the company's ability to realize the vision. He decided to use the company's annual off-site with its top 100 leaders to clarify the company's new vision and gain commitment. Before the off-site, the attendees completed a survey about the company's vision, goals, strategy, employee engagement, and culture. The results indicated that Bolen Technologies was above average in goal clarity but well below average in alignment, engagement, and communication. The findings disappointed Randy because he had spent 18 months communicating the vision in the belief that it would transform the company from good to great. Despite having eight successful quarters in a row and being four times bigger than its nearest competitor, Bolen was floundering, and its troubles were self-inflicted. Randy realized that he needed to turn the ship around but was uncertain about how to proceed.

Buy-In Defined

Buy-In concerns the degree to which leaders and members are *committed* to and *engaged* in team goals, roles, norms, and success. There is a difference between member commitment and member engagement. A United States Marine corporal may be very committed to The Corps and protecting the United States, yet he may not be particularly engaged while walking guard duty at Camp Pendleton. In this scenario the corporal will do the minimum and nothing more. Likewise, team members may be committed to the team and its goals yet not engage in the tasks needed to succeed. The Holy Grail for leaders is to create teams whose members who are both committed to and fully engaged in the tasks needed to succeed,

Team members with high levels of commitment and engagement work toward team goals, take their roles and responsibilities seriously, adhere to team norms, and do what Is needed to help their teams and groups win. The members of teams and groups with low levels of commitment and engagement may publicly agree to decisions but privately ignore them. Bolen Technologies clearly had a Buy-In problem. Randy Smith's new initiatives may have been sound but without the commitment and engagement of his executive leadership team and subsequent layers of management, the new vision could not become a reality.

The members of teams and groups who lack Buy-In are unconcerned with goal achievement. Executive leadership teams want to avoid conflict, so the lack of Buy-In may not be apparent in their meetings. However, when leaders use proxies to fight their battles, a chain reaction of inter-department finger pointing is highly probable: the sales leaders may complain that R&D designs products that nobody wants; leaders in R&D will blame operations for building products with poor quality; both groups will blame IT for poor software systems, etc. Although outside the board room Rome is burning, executive team members are oblivious.

The lack of Buy-In is not confined to executive teams; any team can have members who are not committed to success. Uncommitted and disengaged members focus on their own agendas and blame others when things go wrong. When Buy-in is lacking, leaders hear: "It wasn't my fault," "I got my part done," or "I never agreed with that decision." A clear *Mission*, high levels of *Talent*, and effective *Norms* do not ensure success when teams lack *Buy-In*. Buy-In is the rocket fuel for team success. Just as rockets with more fuel carry heavier payloads, teams with greater Buy-In can achieve more difficult goals.

Buy-In differs between groups and teams. Group members only need to buy in to their individual roles; team members also need to buy in to their team norms and goals, be willing to cooperate and do joint work, and internalize the idea of shared fates. In a group, if members do not have high levels of Buy-In, they may fail to achieve their individual goals, but this may not impact the group's overall success. Teams, however, depend on cooperation and joint work to succeed. Teams with only one or two low Buy-In members (think Slackers or Criticizers) will lose. This difference between teams' and groups' Buy-In has important implications for leaders.

Since Buy-In is a critical component to team performance, how can leaders motivate members to be committed and engaged in team success? There are three techniques that can enhance Buy-In: improving credibility, communicating a compelling vision, and enabling empowerment.

What Role Does Credibility Play in Buy-In?

Interviews with thousands of people and over a million 360-degree feedback ratings show that credibility is a critical component of leader effectiveness and team success.[60, 61] Credibility can be defined as the degree to which members believe in the leader; it has two components—trust and expertise.[62] Trust concerns building strong relationships with others; expertise relates to having the relevant knowledge and skills. Because trust and expertise are independent, leaders and members can have a variety of high and low combinations.

	Low ⟶ Trust ⟶ High	
High (Expertise)	*Untrustworthy Expert* — Has relevant knowledge and skills but needs to build trusting relationships with team members before influencing others.	*Trusted Veteran* — Has the knowledge, skill, and relationships with fellow team members needed to make significant contributions to team success.
Low (Expertise)	*Rookie* — Needs to build trusting relationships and personal knowledge and skills before being seen as credible by others.	*Trustworthy Novice* — Has good relationships but needs to develop relevant skills before being seen as credible by fellow team members.

The fact that trust and expertise are both needed to establish credibility leads to interesting group dynamics. For example, teams often recruit new leaders and members with needed expertise, but their advice may be ignored until the other members begin to trust them. Seasoned veterans who have the required knowledge and skill set but are difficult to work with do not influence decision-making. Leaders who want to improve their credibility need (at least) moderate levels of relevant expertise and team member trust. Leaders must then persuade the team that each member has the expertise needed to perform his or her respective role. Establishing confidence in fellow team members builds trust and enhance group cohesiveness. If any team member lacks credibility, then Buy-In suffers and the team may fail. By gaining the trust of other team members and providing additional coaching or training, leaders can help those players who lack credibility.

Two other aspects of credibility are worth noting. First, leaders must not expect to establish credibility immediately because relationships and reputation for expertise can't be developed overnight. Second, leaders must understand how quickly credibility can be destroyed. If leaders say one thing but do another, if they violate team norms or organizational policies, if they fail to follow through on commitments, or if they lack relevant expertise, then their credibility evaporates. Once lost, credibility is hard to regain. It may be easier to replace an individual rather than try to rebuild the credibility of a team, group, or organization. Applying what we know about credibility to the situation at Bolen Technologies, credibility was probably not the cause of Randy Smith's Buy-In problems. He had the relevant expertise and had spent four years surrounding himself with people he trusted. Something else caused the poor Buy-In of his leadership team.

Can a Leader's Vision Enhance Buy-In?

Some people are gifted orators who can inspire others. Research shows that leaders who paint powerful visions of the future have subordinates who exert extra effort towards team and group goals.[63-66] However, few leaders provide those clear visions for their teams or groups. When asked to describe their vision for their teams, most leaders are either stumped or make lengthy, convoluted explanations. It is ironic that many people who work hard to attain leadership positions cannot explain why anyone should join their teams. When President George H. W. Bush was running for a second term in office, his staff asked him what his vision was for his second term. He responded, "Vision, vision, what is this vision thing?" Most observers believe his inability to articulate his vision cost him the election.

Many leaders would communicate persuasive visions for their teams if they knew how to do it properly—the "vision gap" is a victim of knowledge not motivation. When creating and explaining their visions for the future, leaders need to keep five factors in mind: (1) honor the past, (2) be realistic about the present, (3) provide hope for the future, (4) capitalize on stories and metaphors, and (5) use emotional energy during delivery.

Honor the Past

When honoring the past, leaders should acknowledge the past accomplishments of the team. Many teams and groups have long histories and leaders should begin their vision statements by pointing out some prior achievements. One sales leader began his vision statement by naming the big wins the team had over the past quarter and what members did to make it happen. Although leaders in charge of newly formed teams have no past accomplishments to acknowledge, they can talk about the achievements of the parent organization and how those feats relate to their teams. Honoring the past provides the context for the leader's vision and builds trust with the audience.

Be Realistic about the Present

Pointing out the facts of the current situation, no matter how grisly, is the hallmark of being realistic about the present. Good leaders not only point out the team's strengths but also note shortcomings and challenges. Members typically understand the team's strengths and shortcomings, so pointing out these characteristics improves a leader's credibility. Failing to acknowledge a team's deficiencies erodes a leader's credibility and members' commitment to the vision. A vice-president of operations in the energy industry used a single slide to identify the pluses and minuses for his 22 power plants. Although most of the plant managers were aware of the issues, the slide assured that everyone was on the same page.

Provide Hope for the Future

To provide hope for the future, leaders describe where their teams and groups need to go and what they need to do to get there. This component of vision should provide a picture of the future, the goals to be achieved, and the activities to be accomplished to make the vision a reality. Leaders should articulate clear expectations regarding team member behavior. Finally, they need to create a bumper sticker for their vision of the future. "We will own the heart of the home" is an example of a bumper sticker formulated by the president of a retail brand. Like all good bumper stickers, it clearly defines how the team wins.

Capitalize on Stories and Metaphors

Vision statements also need to capitalize on stories and metaphors. The before-mentioned vice-president of operations used lessons learned by Admiral James Stockdale as a prisoner of war in Vietnam; recounting the Admiral's ordeal, the vice-president described how he wanted his plant managers to lead others.[67] Nothing is worse than listening to people drone on about leadership. Facts tell and stories sell, so leaders need to provide stories or analogies when spelling out their vision statements. Sharing personal lessons learned can help leaders make a stronger case for change.

Use Emotional Energy during Delivery

Finally, the manner in which leaders deliver vision statements can impact team member Buy-In; leaders wanting to fire up the troops need to show emotional energy during delivery.[68,69] Leaders should use about ten minutes and a few slides to deliver their vision statements. If they use more than eight slides or more than 20 minutes, they risk losing interest and member Buy-In. Short, powerful, and personal vision statements gain more Buy-In than meandering academic monologues. Looking back at Randy Smith's vision for Bolen Technologies, it is easy to see that he violated most of the rules for effective vision statements. Even though his vision made good business sense, he communicated it in a way that was guaranteed to lose Buy-In.

What Role Does Team Member Empowerment Play in Buy-In?

Randy Smith's uninspiring vision of the future was not the major reason for his key subordinates' lack of Buy-In. His omission of team member empowerment killed the Buy-In of his direct and indirect reports. Empowerment stands on two legs--delegation and development.[70] Team members feel empowered when they have the freedom to make decisions that fall within their roles and responsibilities, but they become dispirited when they are micromanaged. In the case of Bolen Technologies, Randy Smith worked exclusively with Connie to develop the company's vision. Although his intentions were laudable, he essentially disempowered his top subordinates by cutting them out of the vision-formulation process.

The subordinates' expertise would have contributed to the vision and to the defining of the strategic initiatives; instead, Randy micromanaged his top leaders by telling them what and how they were to get things done without their input.

Leaders can do several things to empower team members. The first step is to ensure team members have clear roles that define the needed knowledge, skills, and decision-making responsibilities. Involving members in team decisions also improves empowerment as members who contribute to the decision-making and create the action plans will have higher levels of Buy-In than those who do not participate in these activities. Involved team members are those most committed to and engaged in team success.

Conclusion

Context describes the situation, *Mission* is concerned with team goals, *Talent* focuses on member roles and responsibilities, *Norms* pertain to the work rules, and *Buy-In* is about commitment and engagement. Groups and teams will achieve little if people are not committed and engaged. To return to the rocket fuel analogy— the more fuel, the bigger the payload. Teams with high levels of Buy-In are more productive than those whose members are not engaged in team or group success.

In many ways the goals to be achieved and the nature of the work to be performed drive the level of Buy-in needed to succeed. Easy goals that do not require coordinated effort also do not need member engagement; hard goals that require joint effort need high levels of Buy-In. To be successful, teams typically need higher levels of Buy-In than groups, which places some unique demands on team leaders. Team leaders need to make a compelling case for why members should work hard and work together; they also need to be alert for variations in member commitment and engagement. Team member Buy-In can fade; subsequently, leaders often need to coach, encourage, and cajole members to stay focused on team success. Setting goals, roles, and rules are discrete events, but keeping members engaged is an on-going challenge.

Buy-In Exercises and Activities

Journey Lines

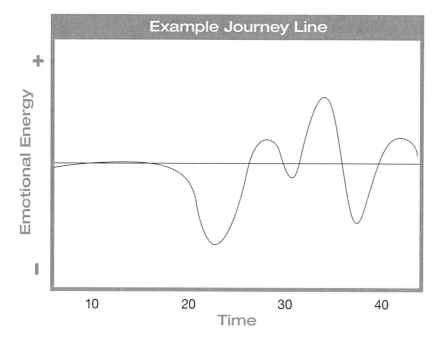

The remainder of this chapter describes two exercises leaders can use to improve members' Buy-In. The journey line exercise is a quick way of fostering credibility by building trust and gaining a better understanding of member expertise. This exercise can also help leaders and members discover where they developed their values, how they learned their most important lessons about work and life, how they recovered from major challenges, etc. The exercise is very useful in the following situations:

- Helping new teams and groups quickly get familiar with members' backgrounds.

- Helping existing teams develop deeper relationships between team members.

- Helping teams understand the key drivers of members' behavior.

The Rocket Model

Objective: To create a journey line for each leader and team member.

Room arrangement: Ideally the room should hold everyone on the team and have enough wall space to post a flipchart for each member.

Time requirement: Approximately 15 minutes per member.

Materials requirement: Flipchart paper, markers, masking tape, Journey Line forms for each member.

Leader Instructions:

1. Leaders should complete their own Journey Line form prior to conducting this exercise as they may do several revisions before sharing it with the rest of the team.

2. Bring the team together and explain that the journey line exercise is a rapid-cycle method for understanding team member experiences and building trust.

3. Draw a blank Journey Line form on a flipchart. Review the emotional energy and time axes and explain the mid-point line represents when things were going okay. Use a different colored marker to draw a line that goes above and below the mid-point line and explain that this represents when things were going well or poorly. Use one or two examples to describe these highs and lows.

4. Give members 10-15 minutes to sketch out their own journey lines using the Journey Line form. Tell members that they should begin by identifying at what point in time they want to start their journey lines and then designating their significant time segments at the bottom of the form. For example, some members start their journey lines at birth and then identify primary and secondary school, college, and the different companies they worked for as their time segments. Others may start their journey lines right after high school and opt for five or ten year increments. It does not matter where people start or what time increments they use. They may also want to use a pencil when sketching their journey lines as they will likely make changes as they work on their forms.

5. After the forms have been completed, give everyone 10 minutes to reproduce their journey lines on flipcharts. Members should write their names at the top and put their flipcharts in landscape mode when sketching out their journey lines. Completed journey line flipcharts should be taped up next to each other on a wall.

6. Because leaders set the tone for this exercise, they should be the first to review the journey line. Begin by telling everyone to share only what he or she is comfortable revealing to others. Leaders should take the next 6-8 minutes to review their personal journey line. Tell members about the key highs and lows, what was learned from these experiences and how they shaped personality and character, etc. Then give members 2-4 minutes to ask questions about the journey line. The extent to which leaders share their personal experiences gives cues to members on what they should share.

7. Ask for a volunteer to go next and give team members 10 minutes to review and answer questions about the journey lines. Be sure to keep track of time as it is easy for people to spend 30 minutes on a single journey line. If a journey line briefing is taking too long, ask people to continue the discussions at a later time and move on to the next member. Repeat this process until everyone on the team has briefed his or her journey line.

8. Wrap up the exercise by asking members what they learned by going through everyone's journey lines and how this knowledge can help team or group functioning.

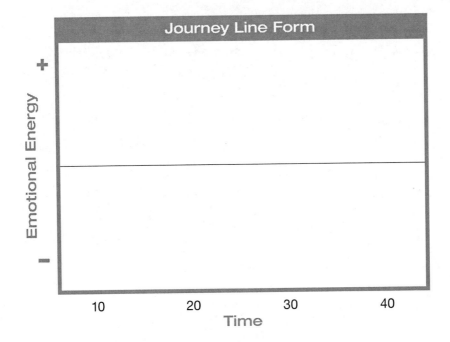

- When was I happiest? Most frustrated? What caused these emotional highs and lows?
- What experiences shaped who I am today?
- What did I learn from creating my journey line?

Vision Statements

Anyone in charge of groups or teams should have a clear and compelling vision statement. Good vision statements provide context, set a direction, describe key activities and expectations, and increase member Buy-In for team and group goals. Vision statements are very useful in the following situations:

- Helping new teams and groups understand what they need to do to win.
- Helping existing teams stay focused on winning.
- Helping new or geographically dispersed members understand where the team is headed and what they need to do to help their team succeed.
- Helping teams and groups determine some of the root causes of dysfunction and conflict.

Objective: To create and deliver vision statements for teams and groups.

Room arrangement: Ideally a room that holds everyone on the team and an LCD projector and screen if the leader is using PowerPoint slides.

Time requirement: Approximately 10 minutes.

Materials requirement: Completed Vision Statement form.

Leader Instructions:

1. Complete the Vision Statement form.

2. If needed, create PowerPoint slides to help communicate the vision statement. Vision statements should be limited to no more than eight slides—the fewer the slides the better. Some of the best deliverers do not use any slides.

3. Create a bumper sticker for the vision. The bumper sticker is a short sentence, saying, or acronym that describes the essence of the vision statement. Leaders may opt to put the bumper sticker on letterheads, t-shirts, posters, or other office accessories to help brand the vision statement.

4. Reading slides is the kiss of death for vision statements, so practice the presentation until the vision statement can more or less be recited from memory. Because past behavior is the best predictor of future behavior, make sure to demonstrate some emotion during the practice sessions.

5. Deliver the vision statement to the group or team. It may be best to deliver vision statements early in a team or group's formation, when an existing team is changing direction, during quarterly or year-end reviews, or when planning for next year. When and where vision statements are delivered can have almost as much impact as the statement itself, so give careful consideration to time and location.

6. Hold a question-answer-reaction session immediately after delivering the vision statement. Ask people what they heard, what they think, and what they feel about the vision statement. Clarify any misunderstandings and end the session by expressing confidence in the team's ability to make the vision become reality.

Vision Statement Form

Honor the Past

What has the group or team done well in the past? Be specific.

Be Realistic About the Present

What is the group currently doing well? Be specific.

Where does the group need to improve? Be specific.

Vision Statement Form

Provide Hope for the Future

Where does the team need to go?

What goals does the team need to accomplish? (How should the team measure success?)

What does the team need to do to accomplish these goals? (How does the team win?)

What are your expectations for team member behavior?

Bumper sticker:

Does the vision statement include stories or analogies?
Where does emotion come into play with the delivery of the vision statement?

[8]

Power—What Resources
Do We Need?

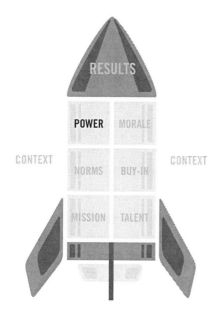

Power Key Points

1. Power pertains to a team's resources.

2. Authority is a critical team resource.

3. Mission drives resource needs.

4. Most teams squander resources.

5. Leaders either make do, lobby for resources, or renegotiate deliverables when Power is lacking.

Kelly is the director of a materials research laboratory in the Department of Defense. Smart and ambitious, she worked in the private sector for nine years before joining the lab ten years ago. Based on her performance, she was put in charge of a team of 12 direct reports and 1,000 employees. Her leadership team consists of a deputy director, seven research department heads, and the heads of finance, IT, facilities, and human resources.

The laboratory's main objective is to develop materials that make military equipment lighter, more durable, harder to detect by radar systems, etc. The laboratory is an international leader in the application of nanotechnology and biomimicry to materials. With facilities to conduct cutting edge research (lesser projects are contracted out to university and commercial laboratories), the lab's staff is dedicated to its mission and takes pride in its work.

Over the laboratory's long history, it has developed materials that are used in government and commercial applications; for example, the lab developed a material that prolonged the life of the military's turbine engines and then sold the process to commercial aircraft manufacturers. The laboratory is always busy because customers are always looking for new materials to solve their operational and maintenance problems. Since most customers want applied solutions (e.g. the U.S. Army wants materials to protect soldiers from IED attacks), approximately 70 percent of the laboratory's annual $500M budget is dedicated to applied research. Nonetheless, Kelly believes that basic research is what establishes the laboratory's reputation as a top-flight research institution, and some of its basic research projects have provided innovative solutions to customers' material issues.

The laboratory's annual budget closely correlates that of the Department of Defense. The wars in Iraq and Afghanistan caused the lab's budget almost to double in the past decade. As the Iraq war came to a close, the Department of Defense was expected to reduce its budget. Kelly was organizing the lab's annual budget planning off-site when she learned that her budget would be cut by $250M—even though she has a large backlog of customer requests.

The laboratory had experienced budget cuts before, and most leadership team members expected a modest reduction in annual funding, but all were surprised at the size of the reduction. A year earlier, the laboratory had started upgrading its facilities and implementing an expensive recruiting program for college graduates with nanotechnology and biomimicry backgrounds. The new budget meant that these projects would create an even larger funding shortfall. What should Kelly do?

Power Defined

The Power component of the Rocket Model is concerned with the quantity and quality of resources available to a team. Resources include facilities, office space, computers, telecommunication systems, specialized equipment, software systems, and budgets—and they are all components of team Power. Power also concerns the level of authority granted to teams. Executive leadership teams often have wide discretion in decision-making—for example, the authority to spend billions to acquire other companies. In contrast, task forces such as the 9/11 Commission[71] or the National Commission on Fiscal Responsibility and Reform[72] can only make recommendations and have little authority to make final decisions.

All groups and teams need resources to succeed. However, the resources that they need depends on their goals. Account executives who are part of a regional sales group need computers, customer resource management software, sales collateral, and travel budgets. To compete successfully, a professional hockey team requires training facilities, hockey equipment, chartered aircraft, etc. Lacking physical resources or the authority to acquire them impedes team and group success. For example, a manager of a talent-acquisition team for a major retailer had to have all staffing decisions approved by three layers of management. Virtually every decision, no matter how small, needed the blessing of a senior vice president of human resources. This bureaucratic structure significantly reduced the team's ability to make timely hiring offers, and they routinely lost highly qualified candidates.

Power is similar to empowerment (discussed in Chapter 7), but it operates at the group rather than the individual level. Individual team members are empowered when they have the skills and authority to accomplish their assigned tasks. Similarly, teams have power when they have the authority to acquire critical resources and become weak when they lack this authority. Even the most powerful teams may have little impact: the National Commission on Fiscal Responsibility and Reform had all the staff, equipment, budget, and access to information it needed to recommend ways to reduce the national debt.[73] However, it was a Presidential commission with no decision-making authority, and the President and Congress ignored its recommendations.[74] Leaders (e.g. CEOs or school superintendents) can and often do ignore the recommendations of their aides or support groups.

Leaders need to clarify their team's or group's purpose before worrying about the Power they need to succeed. Leaders should ask if the team should make recommendations or achieve results. If it is the latter, then how do these results impact the larger organization? Teams that make big contributions need more power than those that make few contributions. Clarifying who makes the decisions about physical assets, budgets, and authority can help improve commitment and cohesiveness; nothing disempowers a group or team faster than discovering that upper management make all the calls.

Key Power Questions

1. How do leaders determine what resources are needed to succeed?

2. Do teams have too many or too few resources?

3. How can leaders cope with Power deficits?

How Do Leaders Determine What Resources Are Needed to Succeed?

Mission is the most important component in the Rocket Model. Mission should determine the number of team members, the team's operating rhythm, the level of commitment required, and so on. Mission also defines the resources and authority a team needs to succeed. The goals of a pacemaker quality-control team versus a retail loss-prevention team are different; as a result, they need different facilities, office space, hardware, authority requirements, etc.

Groups and teams with poorly defined goals have difficulty estimating the resources they need to win. In such situations, leaders often define success in terms of the size of their empires. They constantly maneuver for more money, staff, office space, and equipment although their groups or teams rarely contribute to the larger organization. Examples of empire building can be found in any organization that lacks clear goals: many government agencies, public school districts, universities, and IT and human resources departments. Left to their own devices, these corporate entities become funding black holes that chronically complain about resource shortfalls. Rather than examining their group's internal and external constituencies and using this information to identify clear goals, their leaders will set vague goals that justify the existence of their empires.

Team and group goals never remain static, and neither do the resources needed to achieve those goals. Teams sometimes change direction or finish projects that are smaller than originally planned; if this modification happens, then teams may need to shed assets to make efficient use of resources. These changes may be temporary and the assets may be needed later, but the assets often remain with the teams even when the changes are permanent. Leaders should ensure the team's physical assets and authority are relevant to the team goals.

Do Teams Have Too Many or Too Few Resources?

Teams and groups often complain about a lack of funding or authority, but research shows that most will squander their resources.[75] Consider the money spent rebuilding Iraq and Afghanistan. Billions of dollars are unaccounted for, but governments still plead for more money to rebuild the countries.[76] Few teams or groups have access to this level of funding, but they still fritter away resources. Consider, for example, the money spent on team training. Many groups or teams have a use-it or lose-it mentality about budgets. As a result, many management consulting firms report great fourth-quarter financial results. It is not as if the training needs of teams or groups just happen to emerge at the end of the year; rather, they risk having their training budgets cut if they do not spend their money. The same is true for travel budgets, equipment, and office space. We know many small software development teams whose priorities are sites first, employees second, and company or product development goals third. Teams with these priorities will squander resources.

How Can Leaders Cope with Power Deficits?

Most groups or teams have the resources they need to succeed, but some do suffer from resource gaps. Indeed, the biggest barriers to success are often the lack of funding, facilities, equipment, or authority. In these situations, leaders have three options. First, the leader can simply try to solve the problem. Most managers believe they need more resources to be successful, but the best managers secure results with the leanest of budgets. Necessity is the mother of invention, and the most effective leaders use what they have to achieve success. As an example, a general counsel had his budget cut by 20 percent to help the parent company reduce expenses during the 2008-2009 recession. Nonetheless, the law department met all of its internal customer-satisfaction, employee-engagement, litigation, patent, settlement, and outside counsel expense goals.

A leader's second option is to make tradeoffs or negotiate deliverables. Groups or teams may be able to accomplish their goals if given more time or if customers prefer certain deliverables over others. Asking customers for input when setting priorities or extending deadlines can help build long-term relationships, especially if the customers are given advanced warning about these issues. However, using this option risks customers going elsewhere to meet their needs.

The third option is to lobby for additional resources by appealing to team sponsors or upper management or asking stakeholders to appeal on the team's behalf. For example, the laboratory director at the beginning of this chapter could have lobbied her boss for a smaller budget cut, asked her military customers to contribute funding, or asked customers to appeal to her superiors regarding the laboratory's funding, but lobbying for additional resources can backfire. Peers may become jealous (if they lose resources), bosses and customers can say no to additional resource requests, and bosses can become annoyed when pestered to provide more resources. The odds of blowback can be high, so leaders need to tread cautiously when pursuing the lobbying path.

Conclusion

Power concerns the quality and quantity of the resources that groups or teams need to win. Critical resources might include training facilities, laboratories, vehicles, computers, software, telecommunications gear, office space, and budgets. Resources also include enough authority to acquire the needed resources. A team's goals should determine a team's resources. For example, professional baseball teams have different goals than deep-sea oil exploration teams and, therefore, have different resource requirements. A second criteria for determining the level of resources needed by a team is its impact on the organization's mission or bottom line. Teams with the potential to have a big impact on a company's financial performance or mission need more authority than teams with little direct impact.

Teams with poorly defined goals often generate few tangible results and can be huge drains on organizational resources. Even teams with clearly defined goals can use resources inefficiently. The main cause of waste is leaders not learning to make do with what they have. The best leaders find ways to achieve results despite shortcomings in resources. Leaders who actually lack critical resources can negotiate priorities and deliverables or lobby for bigger budgets and more authority. Nevertheless, leaders should weigh the pros and cons of these approaches carefully as both entail some degree of risk.

Power Exercises and Activities

Resource Analysis Exercise

The rest of this chapter describes two exercises leaders can use to optimize team or group resources. The Resource Analysis Exercise is a systematic process for determining the facilities, equipment, office space, systems, budget, authority, etc. needed by team or groups to succeed. This exercise is very useful in the following situations:

- Helping new teams and groups to quickly determine their resource needs.

- Helping existing teams determine whether they are making optimal use of their resources.

- Helping teams make a case for additional resources.

Objective: To analyze the resources available and those required of a team or group.

Room arrangement: Ideally the room should hold everyone on the team and have enough wall space to post several flipcharts.

Time requirement: 60-90 minutes

Materials requirement: Flipchart paper, markers, masking tape, Resource Analysis Exercise forms for each member.

Leader Instructions:

1. Review the team or group goals with members.

2. Reproduce the Resource Analysis Exercise form on several flipcharts.

3. Pass out the Resource Analysis Exercise forms to members. Work with the team to develop answers for the Need column for each of the categories. Write consensus answers on the flipcharts. (Note: Teams and groups that already have assets and authority in place should try to complete the Need column by assuming they have no resources. In other words, if they were a brand new team with no resources, then ideally what would resources would they need to succeed?)

3. Once all the Need categories have been completed then work with the team to develop answers for the Already Have column for each of the categories. Write consensus answers on the flipcharts.

4. Work with the team to identify the biggest Need versus Already Have gaps.

5. Identify strategies for dealing with the biggest resource gaps. These strategies might include

   - Making do with what the team already has (changing roles and work processes, modifying equipment, developing workarounds, etc.)

   - Negotiating priorities and due dates with customers.

   - Requesting resources (new teams) or lobbying for additional resources (existing teams).

   - Exchanging unneeded resources for needed resources.

6. Create an action plan for bridging the resource gaps. The plan should include specific steps, accountable parties, progress reviews, and a timeline.

7. Assign someone from the group to create an electronic copy of the completed Resource Analysis form and action plan. The documents should be sent out to all members for review and further comment.

Resource Analysis Exercise Form

Resources	Need	Already Have
Equipment: Specialized gear, tools, machines, etc.		
Hardware and software: Computers, servers, programs, data storage, printers, copiers, etc.		
Telecommunications: Land lines, cell phones, faxes, internet access, video conferencing, etc.		
Vehicles: Cars, trucks, specialized vehicles, etc.		
Personal Protection: Fire or hazardous materials protection suits, safety gear, etc.		
Office Space: Offices, cubicles, meeting rooms, storage, etc.		
Facilities: Location(s), security, parking, laboratories, clean rooms, etc.		

Resource Analysis Exercise Form

Resources	Need	Already Have
Service Support: Data access, IT, HR, legal, sales, marketing, quality support, etc.		
Budget: Total dollars, personnel budgets, discretionary and travel budgets, etc.		
Authority: Signing, resource allocation, hiring, firing, decision-making authority, etc.		
Other:		
Other:		
Other:		
Other:		

Stakeholder Mapping

Leaders can use stakeholder mapping to develop strategies for acquiring additional resources. Stakeholder mapping involves identifying all the key influencers, determining the amount of power they have and whether they would be for or against additional resource requests, and then developing plans either to leverage their influence or negate their resistance. Stakeholder mapping is very useful in the following situations:

- Helping new and existing teams acquire needed resources.
- Helping teams drive organizational change.

Objective: To develop strategies to acquire needed resources and work with the team to identify which resources are to be acquired

Room arrangement: Ideally the room should hold everyone on the team and have enough wall space to post several flipcharts.

Time requirement: 90 minutes

Materials requirement: Flipchart paper, markers, masking tape, Stakeholder Map and Action Plan, Attitude x Power Grids, and Suggested Strategies for Stakeholders forms for each member.

Leader Instructions:

1. Review the team or group goals and resource gaps with members.

2. Reproduce the Stakeholder Map and Action Plan and Attitude x Power Grid forms on flipcharts.

3. Pass out the Stakeholder Map and Action Plan, Attitude x Power Grids, and Suggested Strategies for Stakeholders forms to members. Explain that the purpose of the meeting is to develop strategies to acquire needed resources, and work with the team to identify which resources are to be acquired and write them down on the Stakeholder Map and Action Plan form and flipchart.

4. Tell members that stakeholders are those people, teams, or organizations that are affected by the team's success, failure, or requests for additional resources. Work with the team to brainstorm

all key stakeholders. Ask members to write the stakeholders in the appropriate column on the Stakeholder Map and Action Plan forms and flipcharts.

5. Ask members to rate the degree to which each stakeholder would support or oppose the team's request for more resources. Members should use the following rating scale when rating stakeholder attitudes:

    ++ Strongly in favor of granting additional resources.

    +   In favor of granting additional resources.

    0   Neutral in granting additional resources.

    -   Opposed to granting additional resources.

    -- Strongly opposed to granting additional resources.

    ?   Unknown attitude towards granting additional resources.

    Ask members to independently rate each stakeholder's attitudes on their Stakeholder Map and Action Plan forms. Once all the members have done their ratings, work with the team to develop consensus attitude ratings for each stakeholder. Write these in the appropriate column on the flipcharts.

6. Ask members to rate the level of power each stakeholder has with respect to granting additional resources. Stakeholders with high power can provide the team with needed resources; those with low power have little ability to provide the team with needed resources. Members should use the following rating scale when rating stakeholder influence:

    HP: High Power: Can grant the team needed resources.

    MP: Moderate Power: Has some influence over those who can grant resources.

    LP: Low Power: Has little power or influence to grant resources.

    Ask members to independently rate each stakeholder's power on their Stakeholder Map and Action Plan forms. Once all the members have done their ratings work with the team to develop consensus power ratings for each stakeholder. Write these in the appropriate column on the flipcharts.

7. Once all the consensus attitude and power ratings are completed, write the stakeholders in the appropriate boxes on the Attitude x Power Grid flipchart. Ask members to give their reactions to the flipchart results.

8. Have members read over the Suggested Strategies for Stakeholders form and discuss what actions the team should take with each stakeholder. Write the actions, accountable parties, and due dates on the Stakeholder Map and Action Plan flipcharts.

9. Assign someone from the group to create an electronic copy of the completed Stakeholder Map and Action Plan. The plan should be sent out to all members for review and further comment.

Stakeholder Map and Action Plan

Resources to be Acquired:

Stakeholders	Attitude (-- to ++)	Power (LP to HP)	Action Steps/Parties/Dates

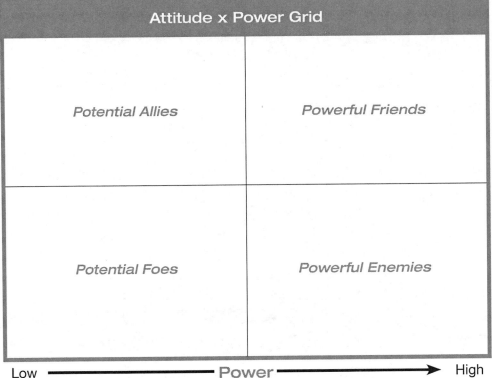

Suggested Strategies for Stakeholders

Potential Allies (Leverage linkages and information)	Powerful Friends (Nuture)
Potential Foes (Keep informed, don't burn any bridges)	Powerful Enemies (Convince, communicate, confront)

Powerful Friends:

- Do not take these stakeholders for granted.
- Get them involved early.
- Get them to leverage their networks and social capital, especially with Powerful Enemies.

Powerful Enemies:

- Do not ignore these stakeholders in your planning.
- Manage conflict with these stakeholders in productive ways.
- Remember that stakeholders who have negative attitudes about the current project may be potential allies on future projects.
- Consider changing the way team goals and deliverables are framed. Be sure that the change in framing is something the team can live with.
- Do not waste social capital unnecessarily.

Potential Allies:

- Do not ignore these stakeholders.
- Keep them informed.
- Ask them to use their social capital and networks, especially with Powerful Enemies.

Potential Foes:

- Keep these stakeholders informed.
- Do not waste social capital unnecessarily or make future enemies of these stakeholders.
- Do not waste resources here that could produce better results elsewhere.
- See whether changing the way team goals or deliverables are framed makes a difference in their response.

[9]

Morale—Can't We All Get Along?

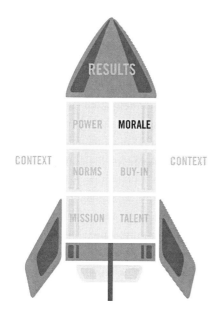

> ## Morale Key Points
>
> 1. Morale pertains to a team's degree of cohesiveness.
>
> 2. Morale is the most observable Rocket Model component.
>
> 3. Most team-building initiatives fail to improve team cohesiveness.
>
> 4. Conflict affects team cohesiveness.
>
> 5. Most teams mismanage conflict.

Telecommunications is one of the biggest variable expenses for large, multi-national companies with annual costs reaching hundreds of millions of dollars. Many organizations see their telecommunication expenses as a black hole—they need it to do business but have no idea how to reduce the costs. Entrepreneurs recognized this predicament as an opportunity and began helping organizations (1) negotiate their telecommunications contracts and service level agreements, (2) determine the lines and equipment being used versus those being charged for, and (3) reconcile telecommunication invoices against contracts. Some telecommunication expense-reduction firms grew to 40-50 person companies with strong revenue streams and healthy margins.

Venture capitalists (VC) soon began to show interest in these firms. One VC firm acquired three companies in six months: Telecontract, a 50-person company that negotiated contracts; Televerify, a 20-person company that did telecom audits; and Telebill, a company of 30 people that reconciled telecom invoices. The VC firm hired Bill, a former CEO and seasoned telecommunication executive, to run the combined firm Savecomm. Bill's job was to increase revenues and reduce costs by integrating the three firms into a single company. This assimilation required implementing an integrated marketing strategy; developing common customer, accounting, and financial platforms; and creating a common Savecomm culture. The VC's goal was to sell Savecomm at a healthy premium in 18-24 months.

Each acquired firm had been successful, and each had a distinctive culture. Telecontract was entrepreneurial with a strong marketing and sales culture. Televerify had an engineering culture, whereas Telebill had an accounting culture. Bill believed that the three existing leaders were proficient at running their separate firms, but he also believed they couldn't take their companies to the next level. Bill replaced them with a select group of people who had worked for him throughout his career. Two or three of these people were competent; the rest were sycophants.

Bill's decision to remove the existing leaders created considerable tension between his new hires and the legacy employees from the three firms. The legacy employees quickly realized that although many of Bill's new hires were incompetent, they were being protected by their relationships with Bill. Then Bill cut the legacy employees out of the decision-making process. The arrogance and condescension of the new hires quickly eroded employee engagement. Six months after Bill's arrival, revenues and margins were declining; systems integration was far behind schedule; and rumors, in-fighting, and backstabbing infested the Savecomm culture. Bill had directed large businesses and always produced results, but the 100-person Savecomm began to look like his career's end. The VC owners were not patient—Bill needed to turn the situation around quickly or he was gone.

Morale Defined

Morale can be defined as a group's or team's cohesiveness or *esprit de corps*. Strong emotional ties, close relationships, and high levels of trust between members are the marks of high morale. Members of high morale teams often say they would do anything for their teammates; in some cases (combat teams or firefighting units), members are willing to die for their units. Conversely, low morale groups and teams, like those in Bill's company, include members who dislike each other and who may sabotage others if doing so furthers their own careers.

Morale is the component of the Rocket Model that is most easily observed by outsiders; it is also the primary reason consultants are asked to do team building.[77] However, team leaders are often unable to assess morale because teams may appear cohesive but have high levels of covert conflict based on norms that require employees to be team players even though they despise one another. The members of these teams smile, nod their heads, and endorse team decisions but secretly resent the process. Leaders need to recognize and deal with this mismatch between members' private thoughts and public actions if they want functional teams.

It is important to distinguish between engagement, cohesiveness, and conflict. As described in Chapter 7, engagement concerns members' willingness to work towards team and group tasks. Members with high levels of Buy-In take their roles seriously and go above and beyond the call of duty when it comes to accomplishing goals. Engagement is quite different from cohesiveness. Highly engaged employees may not particularly like each other, or conversely, members who like each other may not be highly engaged. Conflict is related to but somewhat distinct from cohesiveness. Teams with low or high levels of conflict may not be particularly cohesive. Often the most cohesive teams are those that experience modest amounts of conflict and have developed ways to resolve issues successfully.

Unfortunately, many leaders are unable to ameliorate intra-team conflict. Some hear what they want to hear and ignore the rest. Others know that their teams are riddled with conflict but hope it will just go away. Still others may ask team members to go through team-building activities such as sharing personality test results, golf outings, ropes courses, white-water rafting excursions, etc. One CEO asked his dysfunctional team to go on a one-day sailboat cruise and bring ten objects with personal significance. During the cruise, they were to talk about the objects. Regrettably, many of these personal stories were leaked back to the larger organization and became sources of mockery for certain team members. This story is fairly typical—most team-building events *fail to identify and resolve the sources of intra-team conflict,* and have little if any impact on team cohesiveness.

Team Conflict Continuum

Artificial Harmony	Productive Dialogue	Destructive Conflict
Low	High	Low

Team Morale

This is not to say that all team-building events are pointless—experiential activities can positively affect Morale. However, leaders must choose the right activities, employ them at the right time, and understand how they fit the Rocket Model in order to improve Morale. The causes of conflict and low cohesiveness are often located in other components of the Rocket Model. Members may disagree about the team's internal and external constituencies, goals, roles, norms, resource needs, etc. Identifying and fixing problematic Rocket Model components often improves Morale. Consequently, the direct route to improved team Morale may not be the most effective. Just as kids keep fighting after their parents tell them to stop, team members will continue to fight unless the causes of conflict addressed.

Conflict can be expected whenever people come together. It's important to determine whether the conflict is healthy or unhealthy and how to resolve the disagreements. Managing conflict is critical for team cohesiveness. The graphic above can help leaders better understand how conflict impacts team Morale.

The remainder of this chapter provides additional insights about Morale and actions leaders can take to manage conflict among team and group members.

Key Morale Questions

1. What are the consequences of artificial harmony?

2. How do leaders manage destructive conflict?

3. How can leaders foster productive dialogues?

What Are the Consequences of Artificial Harmony?

No one wants to lead a team that battles with itself and not the competition. Although every team and group (or family) has conflict, society expects that people should coexist peacefully. The demands to get along with fellow employees are even stronger and more explicit in organizations because co-worker affiliation usually affects climate, performance management, and succession planning systems. Organizational expectations that people play nicely are so strong that being unable to do so is a leading cause of managerial derailment.[78-80]

Expectations to get along with others can create odd team dynamics. Many teams maintain a climate of artificial harmony so that controversial issues, difficult topics, and disagreements never come up because members come to meetings with their lips stapled. Although members have misgivings about the group, they don't complain publicly; rather, they express their irritation behind closed doors or at the bar. Leaders need to be attuned to this kind of suppression because they may assume that lack of dissent indicates good Morale. Teams that promote artificial harmony usually display three symptoms. One sign of trouble is having no conflict in team meetings. By contrast, high-performing teams typically experience conflict over solutions, decisions, and future directions. The second symptom is poor execution of team decisions. Execution suffers because, rather than expressing disagreement, members engage in passive-aggressive acts such as turning in late or incomplete work and ignoring the requests of fellow members' team decisions. Another indication of problems is if the company exhibits a "silo" mentality. If harmony prevails at the top of an organization but business units squat resentfully in their silos, then the executive leadership team is practicing artificial harmony.

Artificial harmony drains performance: polite teams get polite results and happy teams are not necessary winning teams. Leaders often prefer fostering relationships to promoting performance which may create teams whose members like each other but achieve less. In addition, many groups or teams set vague or internally focused goals which make it impossible to compare the group's performance with other groups, but it maintains the façade that all is well. This way of evaluating performance makes the members feel good, but the larger organization may be less pleased with their performance (if people actually bothered to look). Polite teams are also likely to squander resources because members never question requests for additional funding.

Mismanagement of conflict can lead to artificial harmony, but the mismanagement of agreement can cause other problems. Groupthink.[81,82] and the Abilene Paradox[83,84] can occur when there is too much agreement. If highly cohesive groups are more concerned with harmony than sound judgments, the members will make riskier decisions than if they decide independently. The Bay of Pigs fiasco, the Challenger space shuttle explosion, and the invasion of Iraq are examples of how groupthink leads to disaster. In all three cases, some members had doubts about the decisions but didn't speak up because their need to belong outweighed their need to make the right decision.

The Abilene Paradox occurs when groups or teams make decisions with which none of the members agree, but people remain silent due to an overpowering need to get along. For example, a team hires someone to fill a critical skill gap. Each team member has reservations about the new hire, but no one expresses any reservations because he or she believes the other team members want to hire the person. After the new hire turns out to be a disaster, team members share their earlier reservations. Both groupthink and the Abilene Paradox can be easily avoided, but only if groups and teams can get beyond faux consensus.

How Do Leaders Manage Destructive Conflict?

The phrase, "This time, it's personal," describes groups suffering from destructive conflict. Signs that a team is not getting along include refusal to talk to or work with other members, displays of personal animosity, development of factions, chronic infighting, backstabbing, and a lack of trust. If the board of directors or executive leadership team is playing Dysfunctional Family Feud, then fratricide will occur throughout the organization.

Groups and teams typically experience a honeymoon period at the start. However, if they consistently lose to competitors, have poorly-defined goals and roles, tolerate a team killer, or establish poor operating rhythms or accountability norms, Morale will collapse, and members will begin to turn on each other. When leaders detect this strife, they often organize a team-building event, but these events provide temporary relief at best because they don't deal with the root causes of the conflict.

If leaders are hired to turn around a dysfunctional team, they need to change the way they try to reduce conflict. The first step is to collect data on team functioning. Leaders can use the components of the Rocket Model to guide one-on-one interviews with members. Leaders can ask each member questions about the team's internal and external constituencies, key assumptions about these constituencies, goals and metrics, member roles, and the operating rhythm. These interviews will enable leaders to determine which exercises would best address problematic Rocket Model components.

Another way to gather this information would be to have members complete a survey that assesses team functioning. The Team Assessment Survey II (TAS II)[85] is a 40-item, on-line survey specifically designed to provide feedback on each of the eight components of the Rocket Model. Examples of feedback provided by the TAS II can be found below:

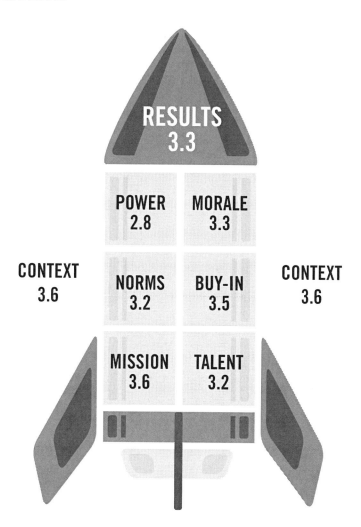

Power

Team Assessment Survey Items () Denotes # of Raters with a <3 Response	
Our team has the authority it needs to make important team decisions.	2.6 (7)
Our team has the equipment needed to achieve our team's goals.	2.9 (7)
Our team has the budget needed to achieve our team's goals.	2.6 (7)
Our team figured out ways to overcome any authority, budget, or equipment shortfalls.	3.3 (2)

Team Distribution

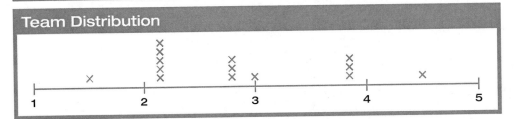

Suggestions for Improvement:

- Devise ways to help the team get the resources and money it needs to accomplish its goals.
- Renegotiate accountables and timelines with customers if the team does not have the resources, money, time, or talent it needs to be successful.
- Work with team sponsors to increase team decision-making authority.
- Use Force-Field Analyses to identify drivers and barriers to change.

As seen in the example, Power is the lowest scoring component for this particular team; consequently, the leader should have the team work through some of the exercises in Chapter 8 to address its Power Issues. However, identifying the causes of team dysfunction and going through exercises to fix dysfunction may not improve team cohesiveness. Leaders must also play the sheriff; they need to ensure that people follow through on the actions agreed upon in the exercises, that the norms are enforced, and that team conflict stays focused on issues and not individuals.

Sometimes teams start out playing nicely, but cohesiveness declines over time. Some leaders enjoy watching members turn on each other, but most are not this mischievous. Rather, many times there is a gap between a leader's intentions and his/her actions, which degrades Morale. A lack of team building know-how also affects team cohesiveness. Many of the lessons leaders have learned from participating in athletic teams or reading books such as The Five Dysfunctions of a Team[86] are wrong. Although leaders truly believe they are doing the right thing, their actions can unintentionally impede team cohesiveness and performance.

So what should leaders do if team Morale begins to drop and in-fighting starts rising? The first step is to bring everyone up to speed on the Rocket Model, which provides a framework for understanding the team's dynamics. The second step is to evaluate how well leaders' actions are aligned with the tenets of Rocket Model. Leaders need to ask whether they have worked with their team to identify the key internal and external constituencies, set team goals and metrics, and clarified member roles and responsibilities. If not, then leaders need to take action to begin addressing the causes of low team cohesiveness.

The third step is to interview members on the Rocket Model components or have them complete TAS IIs, which helps leaders identify the sources of the team's poor Morale and choose exercises to improve team cohesiveness. Leaders should then have the team work through the critical exercises and make them part of the team's regular activities. The final step to improving team cohesiveness is to set clear expectations for member behavior and hold people accountable. Dysfunctional teams need strong sheriffs; if leaders are uncomfortable playing this role, then they will have trouble improving team cohesiveness.

How Can Leaders Foster Productive Dialogues?

We have discussed how the absence of conflict may not be a good indicator of team cohesiveness and how the presence of destructive conflict negatively impacts team cohesiveness. One hallmark of high-performing teams and groups is that they experience some level of conflict so that lively debates and discussions of controversial topics are a regular feature of meetings. Yet, it is the nature of the debates that differentiate highly cohesive and effective teams from their lesser cousins. Teams that are both cohesive and effective focus on solving problems, not attacking other members; leaders and members need to identify what is and is not working on the team but do so in a way that respects individuals. Unlike teams with high levels of artificial harmony, constructive conflict provides an alignment between what people are thinking and actually saying about issues.

So how do leaders make productive (as opposed to contrived or destructive) dialogue part of the communication norm? Leaders who are willing to admit bad decisions and mistakes and to ask for feedback on their performance are taking the first steps to fostering productive dialogue. For example, a group may decide to pursue a certain sales strategy but after three months decide that the strategy is not working. Leaders trying to create a productive dialogue norm might hold a meeting to review the sales strategy. They would then state what they could have done differently to help the team select a better sales strategy. The leader could also ask for feedback on tactical decisions such as assigning accounts to certain team members or implementing a new lead generation process. Leaders who honestly assess their own behavior and ask for feedback eventually put pressure on others to do the same. Once team members realize that they won't be punished for honest inputs, they begin to admit their own misunderstandings and shortcomings about important team issues.

To foster productive dialogues, leaders should ensure that their groups focus on learning rather than assigning blame. Ground rules for creating productive dialogues include publicly stating that the purpose of a meeting is to better understand what did or did not happen, to learn what the team needs to do differently in the future, and to avoid assigning blame. During these discussions, leaders need to be willing to ask probing questions of themselves and others, emphasizing the reason for asking questions is not to play "gotcha" but to help the team avoid repeating mistakes. Most people are defensive and default to blaming others for mistakes; therefore, leaders once again must play the sheriff by redirecting the discussion to the issues at hand when the conversations become personal. Leaders should end these meetings by asking members to articulate what they have learned to create a set of common learnings for the team. Conducted properly, these sessions also improve team Morale.

There are three other points that leaders should remember if they want to increase Morale. First, establishing a productive communication norm won't happen overnight. It takes time for members to have enough trust to share their thoughts about issues. Introducing the productive dialogue concept early helps persuade members to adopt this norm. Leaders will know they have succeeded when members confidently point out areas where the team is falling short, and when discussions stay focused on the issues rather than the shortfalls of individuals.

Second, teams build trust, cohesiveness, and the capacity for further productive dialogue by doing real work such as identifying internal constituencies, setting team goals, passing work between members, acquiring needed resources, and getting tasks accomplished. Conversely, it is hard to have productive dialogues when members are only going through the motions and do not really care about team success.

Third, teams need to have some minimal level of trust for productive dialogues to begin. Leaders can introduce the productive dialogue concept at any time, but some teams are so mired in destructive conflict that they are unable to establish this norm. For such teams, the causes of the conflict have to be identified and addressed before productive dialogues can begin.

Conclusion

Morale, a critical component of team performance, is concerned with a team's level of cohesiveness. Nonetheless, happy teams and groups are not always the most productive: Team members may be very amiable but produce very little work. Unfortunately, many organizations tolerate poor team and group performance. Most teams have goals that are internally focused, goals that don't allow external benchmarking but do encourage navel gazing. For example, many human resources, legal, public relations, IT, finance, marketing, sales, and operations teams can show improvement in their performance when compared with themselves but underperform when compared with similar teams in other organizations.

Morale is an easily observed component of the Rocket Model; it is fairly obvious whether members are getting along or playing Dysfunctional Family Feud, but appearances can be deceiving. Many teams may suffer from artificial harmony (they publicly get along but privately complain about one another). Members often use proxies to express their dissatisfaction with teammates. When artificially harmonious executive teams lead organizations, strong silos and cross-functional in-fighting flourish. Leading teams suffering from low Morale is unpleasant because of the constant backstabbing and tiresome bickering. Leaders need to identify the causes of low Morale and be willing to play the sheriff if they want to turn their teams around.

The biggest challenge for leaders who want to improve cohesiveness is to manage conflict effectively. Teams with no conflict can suffer from artificial harmony, groupthink, or the Abilene Paradox; those with high levels of destructive conflict are often nightmare teams. The most cohesive teams have conflict, but leaders ensure that the debates focus on issues rather than personalities. Leaders can encourage healthy levels of conflict by addressing the causes of team conflict and persuading teams to adopt norms of productive communication.

Morale Exercises and Activities

Team Interview Protocol

The rest of this chapter describes three exercises leaders can use to identify the causes of conflict and create productive communication norms. The Team Interview Protocol is designed to help leaders pinpoint the sources of conflict in teams or groups they are inheriting or managing. This exercise is very useful in the following situations:

- Helping leaders pinpoint to root causes of team and group conflict.
- Helping existing teams identify strengths and areas where performance can be improved.

What follows are the step-by-step instructions for using the Team Interview Protocol.

Objective: To determine the sources of conflict in teams or groups.

Room arrangement: Ideally the interviews should be conducted in a small conference room that affords a high degree of privacy. Leaders should arrange the room so that members are sitting at a small table with the seats placed at a 90-degree angle. The room for the feedback session should be large enough to accommodate the entire team.

Time requirement: 45-60 minutes per interviewee; 120 minutes to analyze and write up the results; and 60-120 minutes for the feedback session.

Materials requirement: Team Interview Protocols for each member.

Leader Instructions:

1. Tell members about the need to do one-on-one interviews to better understand the current dynamics on the team and that their comments will be held in strict confidence, but key themes will be shared at a future meeting.

2. Set up an interview schedule and allow 60 minutes per member.

3. Conduct the interviews. Begin by welcoming the member and reinforcing the rules of confidentiality. State that the purpose of the interviews is to identify areas of strength and improvement opportunities for the team.

Also, say that all members will be interviewed and none of the details from any interview will be shared with anyone else. Use the Team Interview Protocol to ask questions, take notes, and obtain ratings for each component of the Rocket Model.

4. Once all the interviews are complete, compute the lowest, average, and highest rating and analyze the comments to identify top three strengths and top three areas of improvement for each component. Write up the results in a brief report that includes the name of the component; the lowest, highest, and average rating; and the strengths and improvement areas for each component.

5. Review the interview results during a team meeting. Begin by providing an overview of the Rocket Model and then passing out the report. Break the group into four- to five-person sub-teams and allow 30 minutes to identify and flipchart the highest and lowest scoring components, any surprises, and their reactions to the report. Ask the sub-teams to present their findings and have the larger group come to a consensus on the results.

6. Tell members that they will participate in a series of exercises to improve team dynamics and performance. Review the appropriate chapters in this book and complete the exercises that correspond to the greatest areas of improvement with the team at a later date.

Note: Given the authority dynamics between leaders and members, leaders may opt to have a third party do the member interviews, write up the results, and run the feedback session.

Team Interview Protocol

Rocket Model Component	Notes	Rating (1=Low; 5=High)
Context What are the team's most important internal and external constituencies? What are the team's key assumptions and value proposition?		
Mission What are the team's goals? Do the team goals include metrics and benchmarks?		
Talent Is the team sized correctly and does it have the right skills to succeed? Have member roles and responsibilities been explicitly stated?		
Norms Does the team have good meeting discipline? Are team decision-making and communication processes effective? Why or why not? Are all members held accountable for performance? Why or why not?		

Rocket Model Component	Notes	Rating (1=Low; 5=High)
Buy-In Are members equally committed to team success? How can you tell? Do members faithfully carry out team decisions, even if they disagree with them?		
Power Does the team have the authority it needs to succeed? Does the team have the budget, equipment, and systems needed to succeed?		
Morale What is the level of cohesiveness among team members? How does the team handle conflict?		
Results How well does the team create and execute plans to improve performance? How has the team performed compared to its goals? How does the team stack up against other comparable teams?		

Team Assessment Survey II (TAS II)

The TAS II is an online survey that provides detailed information on a team's performance on each component of the Rocket Model. Because the feedback is quantitative in nature, the TAS II can provide teams with benchmarking data. Also since the survey takes less than ten minutes to complete and members' responses are combined with those of other team members, the TAS II avoids some of the time and confidentiality issues associated with the Team Interview Protocol. The TAS II is not appropriate for new teams but is ideal in the following situations:

- Helping leaders pinpoint the root causes of team and group conflict.
- Helping existing teams identify strengths and areas where performance can be improved.

What follows are the step-by-step instructions for administering and providing feedback on the TAS II results.

Objective: To better understand the current dynamics on the team.

Room arrangement: Ideally the room for the feedback session should be large enough to accommodate all members with extra space for sub-team breakout sessions.

Time requirement: 10 minutes to complete individual TAS IIs and 120 minutes for the feedback session.

Materials requirement: TAS IIs administered to all members, including the leader.

Leader Instructions:

1. Tell members that the purpose of doing a TAS II is to better understand the current dynamics on the team. As a result, they will receive an e-mail from Advantis Research & Consulting with survey instructions. Each person's survey responses will be kept anonymous.

2. Send the following information to Gordy Curphy at curphyconsulting@msn.com to have the TAS II administered:

   - Point of contact name, phone number, e-mail address, and regular mail address.
   - Team name.

- Names and e-mail addresses of all team members.

- The date when the feedback reports are needed. (Please allow at least two weeks to administer surveys and generate a feedback report.)

- Name, e-mail, and regular mail address for the feedback report recipient(s).

The cost of the TAS II is $50/participant; therefore, the cost of administering the surveys and generating a feedback report for an eight-person team would be $400 (8 x $50 = $400). The $50/person fee includes a pdf copy of the feedback report. Hard color copies of feedback reports are available for another $20/report plus shipping.

3. Set aside 120 minutes to review the Rocket Model and TAS II Feedback Report during a team meeting. After providing an overview of the Rocket Model, distribute copies of the feedback report and give individuals 20 minutes to review the results. Then break the group into four- to five-person sub-teams and give them 30 minutes to identify areas of strength, areas of improvement, any surprises, and reactions to the report. Ask the sub-teams to present their findings and lead a large group discussion on the implications of the findings.

4. Tell members that they will participate in a series of exercises to improve team dynamics and performance. Review the appropriate chapters in this book and complete the exercises that correspond to the greatest areas of needed improvement with the team at a later date.

Note: Leaders may opt to have a third party run the feedback session.

After Action Reviews

After Action Reviews are a part of the standard operating procedures for the United States Air Force Thunderbirds, The United States Navy Blue Angels and the United States Army Special Forces. The purpose of After Action Reviews is to help these highly trained flying and fighting units identify the lessons learned from past actions and adopt productive dialogue communication norms. After Action Reviews can be used with public and private sector teams in the following situations:

- Introducing new teams to the concept of productive dialogues.

- Teaching existing teams suffering from artificial harmony how to have productive dialogues.

- Helping new and existing teams learn from past actions and avoid making the same mistakes.

What follows are the step-by-step instructions for conducting After Action Reviews.

Objective: To improve team efficiency and effectiveness.

Room arrangement: After Action Reviews should be held in a room large enough to hold the entire group.

Time requirement: 60-90 minutes, depending on the size of the group and issue to be discussed.

Materials requirement: Copies of After Action Review Ground Rules for each member.

Leader Instructions:

1. Identify a major task, milestone, or project for the After Action Review. Ideally this project or task should be something that was recently completed and everyone on the team had a hand in.

2. Set up a 60- to 90-minute meeting to conduct the After Action Review. Send a meeting invitation to all team members stating that the purpose of the meeting is to identify the lessons learned from the recently completed project.

3. Begin the After Action Review by passing out the Ground Rules and describing the purpose of the meeting, which is to improve team efficiency and effectiveness by identifying the key lessons learned from the project. Take no more than 10 minutes to provide some background about the project. This overview might include what the project was about, what key decisions were made, what results were obtained, etc.

4. The leader should state that he or she is going to role model what everyone else will be expected to do in the After Action Review. The leader should then take no more than five minutes to describe

what he or she thought went well and what could have been done differently. It is critical that the leader is brutally honest with the self-assessment as this presentation will set the tone for everyone else.

5. The leader should then ask for specific feedback on what was done well and what could have done differently. If no one offers feedback, then the leader should pick various members to share their perspectives on the leader's actions. For example, the members could be asked if some of the key decisions made or actions taken were effective or could have been done differently. Members should also be asked to provide recommendations for improvement. After hearing all the recommendations, the leader should summarize the lessons learned and thank members for their inputs.

6. Ask for a volunteer to go next. The member should share what he or she did well and could have done differently and then ask other members for feedback and recommendations for improvement. The member should end the session by sharing the lessons learned and thanking the team for their inputs.

7. Repeat the process for the remaining team members.

8. Ask the team to identify the common lessons learned and how they could be applied to on-going projects and tasks.

9. Assign someone from the group to create an electronic copy of the common lessons learned. All members should receive a copy for review and further comment.

After Action Review Ground Rules

1. Focus on learning, not assigning blame.

2. Most people would do some things differently if they had another chance.

3. Before criticizing others, criticize yourself. Self-reflection is critical to learning.
   - What assumptions did you make before taking action?
   - What did you do that helped the team succeed?
   - What part of failure do you own?
   - What would you do differently if you could do it again?

4. Keep feedback focused on actions and behaviors, not personalities or intentions.

5. There should be no sacred cows.

[10]

Results—Are We Winning?

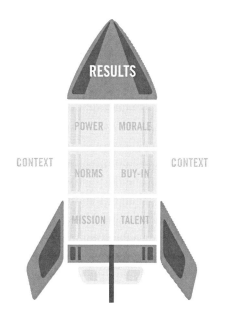

Millicifent, a financial services firm, generated most of its revenue by selling insurance and investment products. The organization was conservative and most of its investment products came from mutual funds rather than securitized mortgages or highly leveraged investments. It successfully weathered the 2008-2009 financial crises; unlike rival companies, it did not need any Troubled Asset Relief Program (TARP) funding and actually gained market share during the economic downturn.

Before the recession, the CEO and General Counsel had a falling out with Millicifent's Board of Directors and were asked to leave. The Board of Directors recruited Mike to be the new General Counsel. Mike had a reputation in the industry for a results-oriented leadership style that included building client relationships, attracting and retaining talent, and advancing business objectives.

When Mike joined Millicifent, the law department consisted of 100 lawyers and their support staff, many of whom had never worked anywhere else. The department was filled with "can't-do" lawyers with excuses regarding why they couldn't help clients. The department put a premium on seniority, getting along with other leaders, and being less demanding than the law firms with which it interacted.

To evaluate the department's norms, morale, and performance, Mike spent time interviewing his eight direct reports, their high-potential successors, and major internal customers. He found that, although the department had 20 percent more staff than law departments in similar financial services companies, customer satisfaction was only mediocre. In addition, the department operated in silos, responded slowly to customers' requests, was not seen as a strategic partner with the business, did not understand the cost of the services it was providing, and did not effectively manage talent. But most importantly, employees did not know what a high-quality law department looked like.

Two months after joining Millicifent, Mike restructured his leadership team. He then held an off-site with his new direct reports where he shared his vision for the law department, honored past accomplishments, described his view of current strengths and shortcomings, and outlined a path to the future. He asked the team to discuss the characteristics of high-performing law departments and review their own customer satisfaction data and budget plans. The team identified its key constituencies, created a scorecard with benchmarks based on high-performing law departments, and defined a new operating rhythm. Mike gave them two months to build strategic partnerships with clients, evaluate talent, and build high-performing teams. Afterwards, Mike held frequent one-to-one meetings with his direct reports, offered advice on becoming strategic partners with their customers, evaluated talent, helped people exit the company or transition into new roles, and worked on improving the leadership team.

Six months later, Mike reduced the law department staff by 20 percent, flattened the budget, and reduced outside legal costs by 40 percent. He noted a 25-percent increase in customer satisfaction and employee engagement, which placed them among the best divisions in the company. In addition, the law department's results continued to improve over time. Mike's changes were so successful that many of his lawyers were promoted into top roles with internal customers or actively recruited by competitors. Mike turned the law department around, but most importantly he taught his direct reports and his employees how to win.

Results Defined

Results are the *what* of teamwork, whereas the seven components of the Rocket Model are the *how* of teamwork. If a team is to compete successfully against others, it must perform at a moderate level on each component of the Rocket Model. Sometimes teams win ugly, in that they produce Results despite a lack of talent or poor norms. Other times teams are just lucky. For example, a team may be dysfunctional but have great products or face weak competitors. Such teams will fail when faced with strong competition. Other teams may lose even though they do everything right. Still others may achieve poor Results due to a single, underperforming component of the Rocket Model, e.g., a team killer, the lack of resources, or poor accountability. Consequently, the relationship between Results and the other components of the Rocket Model is not perfect—some teams do well when they shouldn't and vice versa.

Virtually every significant human achievement has been the result of collective effort, and Results are the reason leaders are compensated. The ability to obtain superior outcomes differentiates effective from ineffective leaders. Most organizations are staffed with managers who don't achieve Results; poor leaders are the biggest obstacles to team or group performance.

This chapter offers some additional insights about Results and suggests some ways that leaders can improve team and group performance.

Key Results Questions

1. What is the relationship between team goals and winning?

2. How do leaders teach teams how to win?

3. What is the relationship between Results and Followership?

What Is the Relationship Between Team Goals and Winning?

Teams win when they achieve their goals, so if a team has ill-defined goals, how can it determine whether it is making progress or has already crossed the finish line? Consider, for example, public schools. If the standards of success have not been defined, public schools cannot know if they are moving the needle. Groups and teams can use SMART-B criteria to build scorecards and define goals that make it easier to measure progress. Teams can choose their goals carefully but still lose; this disconnection happens when teams select internally oriented goals. For example, a human resource department might successfully roll out several employee initiatives and think it has done a great job until an employee engagement survey places the function in the bottom 25 percent of comparable HR departments.

It is easy for teams to win the battles and lose the war. Consider the law department story at the beginning of the chapter—before Mike was hired, people thought the law department was good. However, they never evaluated other law departments and had no metrics to justify their opinion. Only after Mike explained what it meant to be a high-performing law department did people begin to see the light. Many teams look good in practice but fail when they get on the field with competitors.

How Do Leaders Teach Teams How to Win?

A critical but often overlooked role of a leader is teaching the team how to win.[87] Most athletic team coaches and heads of military combat units teach this lesson well; they evaluate the competition and devise strategies and tactics to defeat the opponent. They define team member roles and responsibilities, make members practice, provide feedback and coaching, upgrade talent, and hold members accountable for performance. This regimen is precisely what Mike followed during his first year at Millicifent. He set external benchmarking goals, upgraded his leadership talent, taught his team how to achieve the goals, and monitored progress in accordance with the standards of top-flight law departments. Although it is impossible to know how many leaders follow Mike's example, leaders who don't act like Mike are prone to lead groups and teams that can't win.

Leaders can use three mechanisms to teach their teams how to win. One is to set clear metrics and goals that are benchmarked against the competition. These goals might include market share, survey results, analysts' recommendations, and customer complaints. Given the amount of data available to modern organizations, it is usually easy to find benchmarking information that teams can use to set winning goals.

A second method leaders can use is to review team performance regularly. Periodic team scorecard reviews help members understand where they are succeeding and where they are falling short. These reviews should include discussions about how to improve performance; leaders can also use this time to provide feedback and guidance on proposed solutions.

Creating an action plan is a third way leaders can teach members how win. These action plans need to state the steps members must take to implement solutions, steps that eventually become roadmaps for winning. The best leaders capitalize on all three techniques to drive team performance.

What Is the Relationship Between Results and Followership?

There are some interesting relationships between Results and Followership. First, members can't merely show up and expect to win. Teams composed of Slackers and Criticizers are less likely to win than those composed of Self-Starters. Second, leaders not focused on Results will frustrate the Self-Starters on the team, who will then defect to other teams or turn into Criticizers or Slackers. Eventually the team will reach a point where losing becomes the norm. If teams are allowed to accept losing, any remaining Self-Starters will become demoralized. To prevent this deterioration, leaders need to focus on Results and the people who can help produce those Results. Leaders need to spend time making their stars into superstars and not waste resources trying to turn non-performers into average performers. Leaders who focus on making good performers great, who set external goals for winning, who conduct regular performance reviews, and who ensure action plans are executed will set their teams up for success.

Conclusion

Results are the reason teams exist and leaders are compensated. People working together can accomplish more than individuals working alone. However, many teams underperform when compared to others, and their performance shortfalls are not always obvious. Many groups and teams report improvements month-after-month and year-after-year, but their track records are based on internally benchmarked goals that provide little information on how teams stack up against competitors. Just like bad singers on *American Idol*, many teams believe they are good but can't compete against world-class performers.

Leaders need to do several things if they want their teams to consistently achieve superior results. The first is to pay close attention to the seven components of the Rocket Model. Teams usually need at least modest performance in all the components to effectively compete against other teams; low performance in a single component can sometimes be enough to impact team outcomes negatively. Second, leaders need to instill in their teams the passion and knowledge to win by setting team goals for beating the competition, building clear action plans, clarifying roles and responsibilities, coaching members, regularly reviewing progress, and holding individuals and the team accountable for performance. Third, leaders need to pay attention to the Followership types on their teams. Teams that are populated with Self-Starters, rather than Criticizers and Slackers, are more likely to succeed. Finally, leaders need to realize that their performance is crucial for team achievement. Many leaders ignore Results, the other team components, and Followership types and, in the process, fail to teach members how to win.

Results Exercises and Activities

Team Interview Protocol and Team Assessment Survey II (TAS II)

The rest of this chapter describes four exercises leaders can use to improve team Results. Two of these exercises, the Team Interview Protocol and Team Assessment Survey II (TAS II) can be used in the following situation:

- Helping existing teams identify strengths and areas where performance can be improved.

The step-by-step instructions for using the Team Interview Protocol and Team Assessment Survey II (TAS II) will not be repeated here, as they were already described in Chapter 9.

Force Field Analysis

Force Field Analysis (FFA) is a technique that helps teams systematically examine problems before formulating possible solutions and creating action plans.[88]

The arrows in an FFA are used to depict the forces working for (drivers) or against (barriers) a goal, project, or problem (the longer the arrow—the bigger the driver or barrier). FFAs work particularly well in the following situations:

- Helping new and existing teams understand the drivers and barriers impacting their goals.

- Helping existing teams understand the issues interfering with goal progress.

- Helping new and existing teams build more comprehensive action plans for solving problems, launching projects, or improving performance.

What follows are step-by-step instructions for doing a Force Field Analysis with teams and groups.

Results: Example of a Force Field Analysis

Problem/Challenge/SMART-B Goal: To improve service station operating margins from 8% to 12% by December 2014.

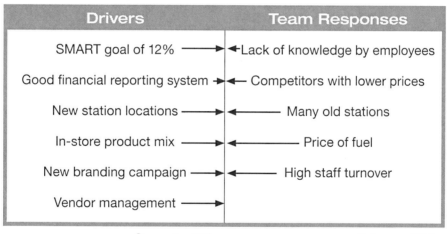

Drivers	Team Responses
SMART goal of 12% ⟶	◀Lack of knowledge by employees
Good financial reporting system ▶	◀ Competitors with lower prices
New station locations ⟶	◀ Many old stations
In-store product mix ⟶	◀ Price of fuel
New branding campaign ⟶	◀ High staff turnover
Vendor management ⟶	

Current = 8%   Future = 12%

Room arrangement: The room should be large enough to accommodate all members.

Time requirement: 30-90 minutes, depending on complexity of the goal, project, or problem to be analyzed.

Materials requirement: Flipchart paper, markers, masking tape, and example FFA handouts for each member.

Leader Instructions:

1. Tell members that the purpose of an FFA is to better understand a problem or challenge facing the team. Use a flipchart to describe the drivers and barriers of a problem the team faced in the past or review the example FFA with the team. Explain that the size of the arrows represents the magnitude of the drivers and barriers, and that the drivers and barriers affecting current performance should more or less balance out. In other words, the current level of performance represents a standoff between drivers and barriers.

2. Tell members that to improve performance, they either need to add or increase drivers, or remove or reduce barriers. Members should also be told that it is often easier to see improvement by removing or reducing barriers than by increasing drivers. Ask the group for ideas on what they could do to increase drivers and reduce barriers to the problem depicted on the flipchart or in the example FFA.

3. Work with the group to identify the problem, project, or goal to be analyzed using an FFA. Make sure the current state and desired future state are clearly defined.

4. If the team has more than six people, then break into three- or four-person sub-groups. Ask each sub-group to use a flipchart to diagram the problem using an FFA. The sub-groups should begin by defining the current and future states, then list the drivers and barriers, and conclude by determining the size of the arrows assigned to each.

5. Sub-groups should use another flipchart to list their recommended actions for moving from the current to desired future state. These actions should either help to increase drivers or reduce barriers.

6. Each sub-group should present its FFA results and recommended actions. Next, the larger group discusses, debates, and decides on a final set of recommended actions.

7. Assign someone from the group to create an electronic copy of the final set of recommended actions which should be used as input to a team action plan.

Team Action Plans

Team Action Plans provide detailed roadmaps for implementing solutions to team problems. They include specific activities/sub-steps, accountable parties, due dates, and completion status, and each should be reviewed as part of a team's operating rhythm. Bigger and more complex problems often require more detailed plans, so doing FFAs beforehand can help ensure all the major recommendations are included. Team Action Plans can be useful in the following situations:

- Helping new and existing teams build roadmaps for achieving goals and solving problems.

- Clarifying the roles and responsibilities of team members.

- Creating a team accountability norm.

What follows are step-by-step instructions for creating Team Action Plans.

Room arrangement: The room should be large enough to accommodate all members. Breakout rooms may be required if sub-groups work on separate action plans.

Time requirement: 30-90 minutes, depending on complexity of the plans.

Materials requirement: Flipchart paper, markers, masking tape, and example Team Action Planning Forms, blank Team Action Planning Forms and Checklists for each member.

Leader Instructions:

1. Pass out the example Team Action Planning Forms, blank Team Action Planning Forms, and Checklists. Announce the project, problem, or goal for which the team will build an action plan. Go over the example Team Action Planning Form and explain how they can use the Checklist to ensure the plan conforms to best practices.

2. Tell members that they should begin with the end in mind—what does the end result look like and when does it need to be completed? They should write this information on the top of their Team Action Planning Forms.

3. Tell members it is usually best to write down the major activities, the sequence for completion, and due dates before determining the sub-steps and accountable parties.

4. If there is only one project or goal to work on, then it is usually best to create the action plan with the entire team. If the team has more than one project or task, then assign them to three- or four-person sub-groups. Ask each sub-group to complete a Team Action Planning Form for their assigned project and use the Checklist to ensure it conforms to best practices. Once the Checklist has been completed, sub-groups should then create a flipchart of their action plan.

5. Each sub-group should present its action plan. Next, the larger group discusses, debates, and decides on the final plan for each goal, project, or problem.

6. Assign someone from the group to create an electronic copy of the final action plans, which should be sent out to all members for review and further comment.

7. Meet with members regularly to review plan progress. The action plans should be living documents with major activities, sub-steps, due dates, accountable parties, and completion status updated as needed.

Results: Example of a Team Action Planning Form

Problem/Challenge/SMART-B Goal: To improve service station operating margins from 8% to 12% by December 2014.

Major Activities/ Sub-Steps	Due Date	Accountable Parties	Completion Status
1. Communicate operating margin strategy to all employees.	Feb 1	Steve	Done
– E-mail with margin goal and rationale sent to all employees.	Jan 7	Steve, Marty	Done
– District Manager briefing kits prepared and distributed.	Jan 7	Marty	Done
– District Manager meetings held with all Store Managers.	Jan 14	Jen	Done
– Store Manager meetings with employees.	Jan 21	Jen	Done
– Town Hall meetings with all employees.	Jan 28	Steve	Done
2. Upgrade the 6 oldest stations.	Jun 1	Mitch	In Progress
– New store design finalized.	Jan 21	Mitch,Steve	Done
– Remodeling vendor selected.	Feb 15	Mitch,Steve	In Progress
– Remodeling schedule finalized.	Mar 15	Mitch,Steve	In Progress
– Remodeling completed.	May 15	Mitch,Steve	In Progress
– Stations restocked and fully operational.	Jun 1	Steve,Jen	In Progress

The Rocket Model

Team Action Planning Form

Problem/Challenge/SMART-B Goal:

Major Activities/ Sub-Steps	Due Date	Accountable Parties	Completion Status

Team Action Planning Checklist

☐ The problem/project/goal and final deadline have been clearly defined.

☐ The major activities have been defined and properly sequenced.

☐ The sub-steps have been defined and properly sequenced.

☐ Realistic due dates have been assigned to all activities and sub-steps.

☐ Individuals have been assigned accountability for each activity/sub-step.

☐ Completion status is up-to-date and accurate.

☐ The plan is realistic—the team has the resources, budget, time, and people needed to complete the plan (or has devised ways to secure needed weak points).

☐ Periodic status reviews have been built into the plan.

☐ The plan is adjusted as needed and any changes have been communicated to all affected parties.

[11]

Putting It All Together

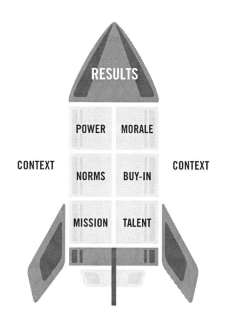

So far we have described the differences between groups and teams, the benefits of the Rocket Model compared to other team-building frameworks, and provided practical exercises for improving the eight components of the model. However, we have not described how leaders actually use the Rocket Model. When leaders use the Rocket Model for the first time, they frequently have the following questions:

- How is the framework used to launch new teams?
- How can the model be used to improve the performance of existing teams?
- How does the model apply to virtual or global teams and groups?
- What are the common mistakes made when using the Rocket Model, and how can they be avoided?

To build a high-performing team or group requires both science and art. The Rocket Model is based on eight years of scientific research. Every aspect of the model (e.g. the framework, exercises, activities, and assessments) has been field-tested and refined with hundreds of teams over the years—and will be further refined as the model is used with more teams and groups. The instructions for the exercises are intended to help with the art of team building, an art that includes implementing and facilitating activities for groups. Just as people can develop appreciation for food by taking cooking classes and trying out new recipes, leaders can also develop their talent for building teams by reading this book and utilizing the exercises. Accordingly, the focus of this chapter is to improve leaders' *artistic* qualities. Leaders with more knowledge and experience using the Rocket Model are better at improving team performance than those who only improvise.

It is worth mentioning a few caveats regarding the use of the Rocket Model. First, leaders must become familiar with the model: the better leaders understand the framework, the better they are able to use it. Second, leaders need to understand what they are trying to accomplish before using a particular exercise with their teams. Leaders can use the exercises in this book in a variety of situations. However, at the end of the day, leaders must ask whether they are using the exercises to help their teams perform at higher levels or because they think the exercises will be fun. Effective leaders use the Rocket Model strategically. They understand that the primary use of the different activities is to improve team functioning, not to give them something to do at a mandatory team-building event. Third, implementation requires time: practice makes perfect. The more leaders who use the TAS II, determine the assumptions for internal constituencies, build team scorecards, do followership scatterplots, set new operating rhythms, deliver vision statements, build stakeholder maps, conduct after-action reviews, and create team-action plans, the better they will be able to achieve results. The remainder of this chapter shows how to use the Rocket Model.

Key Questions

1. How can leaders use the Rocket Model to successfully launch new teams?

2. How can leaders use the Rocket Model to improve the performance of existing teams?

3. What are the key lessons learned from using the Rocket Model?

How Can Leaders Use the Rocket Model to Successfully Launch New Teams?

William was Vice-President of Product Development at a large high-tech company. He had a Master's degree in Applied Physics and 15 years of software development experience; prior to becoming vice-president, he had turned around a $300M software product. Although the product was a flagship offering, it experienced persistent feature creep, quality issues, and timeliness problems that eroded market share and created unfavorable write-ups by industry analysts. William rectified these problems by setting clear goals for quality, on-time releases, revenues, and market share; upgrading and restructuring his leadership team; clarifying roles and responsibilities; instilling a new operating rhythm and accountability norms; teaching the team how to win; and keeping the focus on results. The results of these efforts were quite substantial—revenues, margins, market share, customer satisfaction, and analysts' recommendations all improved substantially.

As William was turning around the product, the company's strategy, marketing, and technology departments identified a significant business opportunity in cloud computing. Each department understood the size of the opportunity and how cloud computing would add value to customers. Subsequently, William was asked to lead the Appliance & Cloud Organization (ACO). The ACO's goal was to develop the next generation of software and hardware. Within six months, he needed to assemble a leadership team and create the business model as well as develop and sell products. William was given a budget and told to achieve $20M in revenues and 30-percent margins by the end of the first year, and $100M in revenues and 40-percent margins by the end of year two.

William was looking for another challenge and taking over the ACO seemed the perfect fit. The project would be visible because the CEO was personally interested in it, but the products were also key to the company's growth strategy. William had never led a start-up and wanted the leadership team to start off on the right foot to reach its targets. Discussions with the marketing, strategy, and technology departments revealed what the new products needed to do. Using this information, he recruited eight people for his leadership team. These people were among the best in the company with backgrounds in software architecture and engineering, project management, quality control, customer service, marketing, and sales.

William knew it would be some time before the team could operate at a high level, and getting them to work together effectively was one of many steps he needed to take to achieve the yearly goals. He not only had to teach his direct reports to work as a team, but he also needed to teach them how to win and create their own high-performing teams.

William designed a series of off-sites for his staff and their groups. The purpose of the first session, which included William and his leadership team, was to help the team understand William's vision and to make certain everyone was on the same page regarding the Context surrounding the ACO. The group also received an overview of the Rocket Model and began working on some of the components which included (1) identifying the ACO's internal and external constituencies and underlying assumptions, (2) creating an ACO scorecard, (3) building a roles-and-responsibility matrix, (4) setting an operating rhythm and (5) constructing action plans to evaluate their progress on the ACO goals. The team agreed to meet weekly to review progress, share information, identify roadblocks, and develop solutions.

Off-Site II took place six weeks later and lasted one-and-a-half days. The purpose of the second off-site was to review the progress made from Off-Site I and help the staff become a high-performing team. Some of the activities in Off-Site II included an in-depth ACO scorecard and action-plan review of one of the major projects; setting communication, decision-making, and accountability norms; and determining ACO resource requirements. The team also created a set of action plans for the next six weeks, including roadmaps for evaluating progress on scorecard goals and hiring needed staff. Again, the team continued to review progress weekly and resolve issues.

Off-Site III took place 12 weeks after Off-Site I; the leadership team met on the first day and were joined by their direct reports on the second day. During the first day, the team reviewed their scorecard and action plans and identified the major barriers to success. For example, one barrier concerned selecting a hardware manufacturer in China; another involved establishing a software development group in India. The leadership team also carried out Force Field Analyses, built action plans for these issues, and prepped for the next·day's session where each team member would be responsible for facilitating parts of that session.

The second day of Off-Site III involved almost 40 people; many of whom were from India, China, and Europe. After the group listened to William's vision for the ACO, they were asked what the vision meant for their groups. William explained the Rocket Model, noted that the leadership team was on its way to becoming a high-performing team, and remarked that he expected the other groups to operate in a similar fashion. One member of the leadership team ran the Context session that featured a review of the internal and external constituencies and their key assumptions. Another leadership member ran the Mission session that reviewed and recommended changes to the ACO scorecard. The leadership team and their respective staffs then met for several hours to build their own scorecards, roles and responsibility matrices, operating rhythms, and action plans.

New Team Off-Site Schedule

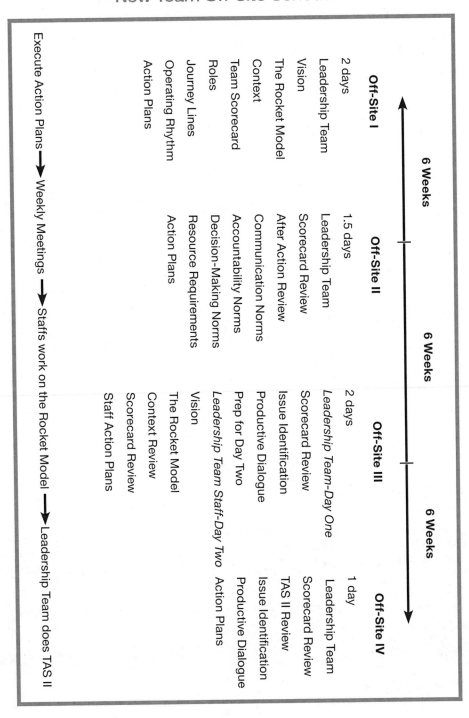

6 Weeks   **6 Weeks**   **6 Weeks**

Off-Site I

2 days

Leadership Team
Vision
The Rocket Model
Context
Team Scorecard
Roles
Journey Lines
Operating Rhythm
Action Plans

Off-Site II

1.5 days

Leadership Team
Scorecard Review
After Action Review
Communication Norms
Accountability Norms
Decision-Making Norms
Resource Requirements
Action Plans

Off-Site III

2 days

Leadership Team–Day One
Scorecard Review
Issue Identification
Productive Dialogue
Prep for Day Two
Leadership Team Staff–Day Two
Vision
The Rocket Model
Context Review
Scorecard Review
Staff Action Plans

Off-Site IV

1 day

Leadership Team
Scorecard Review
TAS II Review
Issue Identification
Productive Dialogue
Action Plans

Execute Action Plans ➔ Weekly Meetings ➔ Staffs work on the Rocket Model ➔ Leadership Team does TAS II

During weeks 12-18, William met weekly with the leadership team and asked them to complete TAS IIs. He also met with individual leadership team members and sat in on some of their team meetings to review progress, provide advice, and help each team understand what it needed to do to win. In Off-Site IV, the leadership team reviewed scorecards, action plans, and TAS II Feedback Report results. The analyses revealed problems establishing the India software team and the need to improve Talent and Norms. More specifically, they found no clear ownership for several issues that cut across sub-teams, which meant that roles, responsibilities, and handoffs needed adjustment. The leadership team adopted longer weekly meetings and quarterly off-sites that focused on reviews of action plans and scorecards, and they implemented a yearly off-site with indirect reports to formulate strategy, update constituency assumptions and scorecards, set budgets, drive alignment, etc. Over the next three months, each member of the leadership team also conducted TAS IIs with his or her respective teams to assess and improve team functioning.

Although the four off-sites and follow-up work were costly, the return was significant. The ACO started selling products after six months and generated $20M in revenues in its first year. Margins and customer satisfaction ratings also met expectations, and industry analysts were pleased with the first round of products. The second year proved equally fruitful. The ACO continued to improve its existing products, introduced several new products to its portfolio, and signed up a number of new channel partners. William was eventually recruited by a competitor, but because his leadership team was aligned, there was no doubt about where the ACO was going and what it needed to get there. The organization subsequently achieved its $100M revenue goal. A more-detailed description of the pre-work, goals, roles, and agenda for Off-Sites I-IV can be found at the end of this chapter.

How Can Leaders Use the Rocket Model to Improve the Performance of Existing Teams?

Frank spent six years in the U.S. Navy as a boiler operator before joining Enerwaste 20 years ago. Enerwaste operates 30 power plants that convert commercial, industrial, and residential trash into electricity, steam, and recycled metals. The company is an environmentally friendly alternative to landfills and traditional power plants; with only ten percent of its trash going into landfills, it produces much lower emissions than coal-fired plants. Frank spent his career at the company's Morton plant, a facility that burned 1,500 tons of trash each day and generated the power for 40,000 homes. Frank joined Enerwaste as a mechanic and moved through many positions before becoming the plant manager five years ago.

The Morton plant had 55 full-time and contract employees. Most of the 12 mechanics worked the day shift but were sometimes called in at night to keep the plant online. There were also five operational shifts that worked rotating 12-hour schedules. Each shift consisted of a shift supervisor, a crane operator, two assistant plant operators, two plant operators, and a control room operator. The plant also had a maintenance manager to oversee the mechanics, an operations manager to oversee the shift supervisors and their staffs, a safety manager, an environmental compliance manager, a controller and several other financial staff, two scale house operators, and eight laborers and administrative personnel.

The plant had several long-term energy contracts that created record revenues and margins. However, three years after Frank took over, these contracts ended and the plant began selling energy on the spot market. Then the energy market virtually collapsed with the advent of fracking technology and the discovery of new natural gas reserves. Revenues and margins dropped over 30 percent despite the plant's "Best in Fleet" awards for operating efficiency, safety, and environmental compliance. Because Frank had little control over revenues, he needed to control costs, maintain operational excellence, and meet the plant's safety and environmental compliance goals. A number of personnel changes made achieving these goals difficult; he lost his operations, maintenance and safety managers (retired, joined another plant, and placed a different position), and half of his direct reports were new to their jobs. Frank realized that the only way for the plant to succeed was to create a high-performing team.

The plant operated 24/7; the safety, environmental compliance, finance, and maintenance groups worked days and the operations staff worked rotating 12-hour shifts. The shifts were configured so that the entire leadership team could get together once every six weeks. Frank decided to use these windows of opportunity to run a series of six team-building sessions. Each session lasted one day, included all ten of his direct reports, and took place in the plant conference room.

Frank used Session I to help his direct reports understand the components of high-performing teams, review the current level of team functioning, gain alignment on internal and external constituencies, and review the rationale for the plant scorecard. Frank asked his direct reports to complete TAS IIs and participate in a 45-minute interview with Amy, the local human resources manager. Amy utilized the Team Interview Protocol and summarized the results for each Rocket Model component in a five-page report.

Session I began with Frank's vision of the plant—where it had been over the past 20 years, where it currently stood, and where he wanted it to go over the next three years. He reviewed the Rocket Model and explained to the group how they would use the framework to become a high-performing team.

Morton Power Plant TAS II Results

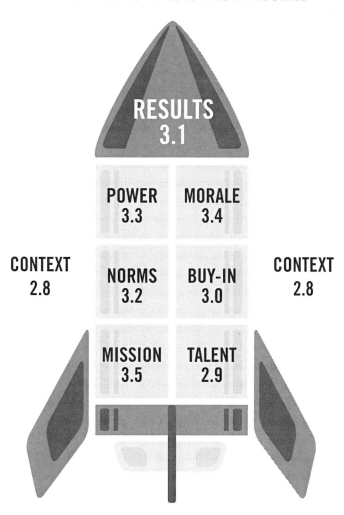

The group then reviewed the results of the TAS II and team interviews; the review revealed room for improvement in every component of the model. After discussing the results, Frank asked the group to identify the plant's primary internal and external constituencies and their underlying assumptions for the next year. Many direct reports found this analysis revealing because they had no idea how the economic downturn negatively impacted trash (i.e., fuel) availability and how the energy spot market affected revenues and margins. The team then reviewed the plant scorecard and discussed what they could do to achieve the plant's goals. The session ended with the direct reports briefing their respective teams on the plant's constituencies and scorecard results.

In the six weeks between Sessions I and II, the direct reports briefed their teams in their morning meetings. These meetings provided a forum for the direct reports to relay information to and receive feedback from their teams. Session II concerned finding ways to resolve recent safety violations. Frank persuaded members to discuss the safety incidents. Although there was no productive dialogue about what happened, Frank convinced the staff to adopt new processes to prevent future safety violations. This discussion rolled into the creation of a roles and responsibility matrix so that members understood who was responsible for the safety incidents. They also discussed accountability norms and built action plans to improve safety.

The morning meetings continued over the next six weeks. Session III reviewed the progress made on the plant goals and safety action plan. Frank reviewed the safety action plan and discovered that the operations and safety managers had not completed their action items. Both managers apologized to the group and promised to do better in the future. Frank then introduced the concept of Followership and had the team do scatterplots and briefings on the followership types for their respective teams. The team had lively discussions about the followership types, and supervisors and managers gained information about their employees (both good and bad) that they had never heard before. Based on this discussion, direct reports identified a person on each of their staffs who could be converted to a Self-Starter; then, they built relevant action plans for making this transition happen. The team also spent time discussing problems facing the plant and building action plans to resolve the difficulties. The session ended with members agreeing to brief their teams on the meeting highlights and carry out their assignments from the action plans.

The daily operations and maintenance meetings continued; Session IV concerned setting new norms for the plant. The session began by reviewing the plant

Existing Team Session Schedule

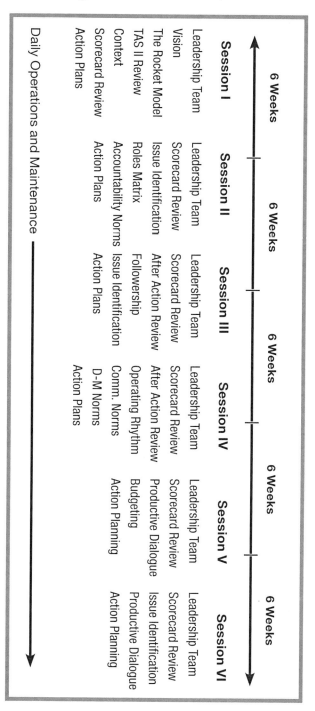

	Session I	Session II	Session III	Session IV	Session V	Session VI
	Leadership Team	Leadership Team	Leadership Team	Leadership Team	Leadership Team	Leadership Team
	Vision	Scorecard Review	Scorecard Review	Scorecard Review	Scorecard Review	Scorecard Review
	The Rocket Model	Issue Identification	After Action Review	After Action Review	Productive Dialogue	Issue Identification
	TAS II Review	Roles Matrix	Followership	Operating Rhythm	Budgeting	Productive Dialogue
	Context	Accountability Norms	Issue Identification	Comm. Norms	Action Planning	Action Planning
	Scorecard Review	Action Plans	Action Plans	D-M Norms		
	Action Plans			Action Plans		
	6 Weeks	6 Weeks	6 Weeks	6 Weeks	6 Weeks	6 Weeks

Daily Operations and Maintenance

scorecard and the prior assignments. Frank continued to emphasize that the purpose of the reviews was learning and continuous improvement, not retribution or punishment. He noticed that the level of candor improved with each review, and the direct reports were now volunteering ways they could improve. They were also asking each other tough questions (some more brutal than Frank would have asked), and occasionally Frank had to keep the group focused on issues. Nonetheless, the team was beginning to have productive dialogues. The session also involved updating the team's operating rhythm, communication, and decision-making norms and creating an action plan for an upcoming maintenance outage. As with previous sessions, members briefed their teams on the new norms and outage action plans while ensuring that the assignments were being carried out.

Session V was used to review how well the operating rhythm changes were working and the lessons learned from the plant outage. The plant was also beginning its annual budget planning process; consequently, much of Session V involved discussing the key milestones in the procedure: setting initial goals for the next year, determining plant priorities and resource needs, and establishing action plans to gather the information needed to create a plant budget. Half of the team had never been involved in the budgeting process, so seeing how the assumptions, goals, trash and energy revenues, maintenance and materials spend, operational results, and staffing issues came together was illuminating for many of Frank's direct reports.

Session VI was held 30 weeks after the first session. The new operating rhythm suggested that the team needed to meet every six weeks to review the plant scorecard and action plans, as well as resolve the strategic issues affecting the plant. Frank led the scorecard review by reminding everyone that in order to win they need to "control the controllables." Although the plant personnel could do nothing about energy and recycled metals pricing, they could ensure that the plant operated efficiently, contained costs, and complied with safety and environmental regulations. Frank asked the controller to lead the discussions on finalizing the plant budget, and the operations and maintenance managers to guide the discussions on preparing for the next maintenance outage. Both meetings were candid, and Frank kept everyone focused on the controllables rather than blaming corporate leaders for setting tough budget numbers.

As Session VI ended, Frank thought his direct reports were operating effectively as a team. Scorecard results were excellent for operating efficiency, preventative maintenance, unplanned maintenance outages, overtime spending, safety, and environmental compliance; these positive reports were supported by a TAS II carried out eight months after Session I that revealed a one point improvement across all eight Rocket Model components. Because power plants are complex operations, the leadership team continued to face challenges, but the members had learned how to work together to solve problems. Most importantly, they had learned how to win, as illustrated by their winning the "Best in Fleet" award for outstanding plant performance for the next two years.

What Are the Key Lessons Learned from Using the Rocket Model?

We have used the Rocket Model with hundreds of teams and groups in many organizations. We have learned six lessons that leaders can apply to their own teams and groups to take full advantage of the Rocket Model. These lessons are not all-inclusive, but they represent important lessons for improving team and group performance.

Lesson 1: Planning and Preparation Is Essential. Winston Churchill once said, "Plans are worthless, but planning is essential." In the two team building examples described earlier in this chapter, an abundance of planning went into each off-site session. William and Frank carefully chose the sequence of activities in their team meetings. William had a new team and followed the linear sequence of the Rocket Model components beginning with setting the Context, defining the team's Mission and developing Talent and so on. In planning for Off-Site I, William spent two hours mapping out the goals, roles, and agenda for the session, spent 90 minutes scripting out and practicing the delivery of his vision for the ACO vision, and spent four hours arranging the off-site logistics, sending pre-work, reviewing the exercises, and assembling handouts. All in all, William spent a day planning and preparing for Off-Site I and similar amounts of time planning and preparing for the other three off-sites.

On the other hand, Frank's team had some prior history, so he was he was able to use the TAS II and interviews to diagnose team functioning. With existing teams, the best places to intervene are usually the lowest scoring components of the Rocket Model, but the Morton plant leadership team had fairly low scores across all eight components, which meant that Frank needed to attend to the Context and Mission components before he could start on any of the other parts. Frank spent four hours reviewing the TAS II and interview results; determining the goals, roles, and agenda;

sending out the pre-work; making logistical arrangements; refining and practicing his vision for the plant; reviewing the exercises; and assembling handouts for Session I. On average he spent similar amounts of time planning and preparing for each of the other sessions.

The bottom line is that leaders who want their teams and groups to perform at higher levels must spend time working on team functioning; making the most efficient use of this time requires planning and preparation. Leaders who do not pay attention to team *functioning* are likely to accomplish little in their team-*building* sessions.

Lesson 2: Improving Team Performance Takes Time and Persistence. Building high-performing teams and groups does not happen overnight—it takes time for people to understand the situation, what needs to be accomplished, what they need to do to win, how they will work together, etc. Teams need to spend time to make time. Setting aside time to work through the Rocket Model usually speeds up execution and helps teams realize results more quickly than if they just plug away at day-to-day issues. These set asides do not need to be formal off-sites or team-building sessions—they can be one- or two-hour affairs that are tacked on to regular group meetings. Calling time-outs to review and craft strategies for dealing with the issues at hand (be they internal or external) can help improve team and group performance.

Leaders need persistence to build high-performing teams and groups. It was six months before William's and Frank's teams began to perform well. Although they had a number of emergencies, they did not get distracted by the *crises du jour*. Leaders who flit from one crisis to another are unlikely to build high-performing teams and groups.

Lesson 3: Capitalize on the Team's Natural Rhythm Whenever Possible. Most teams and groups have a natural working rhythm that leaders can use for team-building sessions. For example, at the Morton plant there was one day every six weeks when all the members of the leadership team were available. Likewise, for many sales teams, the first month of every quarter is a good time to have these events; the summer works for teams in primary, secondary, or higher education; and February and March work for many retail teams. Taking advantage of lulls in activity levels helps members stay focused at the team-building sessions.

Lesson 4: The Rocket Model Can Help Global and Virtual Teams. There are differences in leading local teams versus global and virtual teams: time zone differences, cultural differences, and little face-to-face interaction make communication and decision-making difficult. Moreover, the concept of first team is even more important with global and virtual teams because those working in remote locations often believe their site comes first and that the global team to which they belong ranks lower in their priorities. Given these challenges, the Rocket Model can be helpful to those in charge because it provides a common framework for discussing how to work together. Leaders can use the model to discuss the first-team concept, identify the key internal and external constituencies at the different locations, create a common team scorecard, clarify roles and responsibilities, create an operating rhythm that works for everyone, and set communication and accountability norms for the entire group. Although it may be expensive, we recommend that leaders in charge of global or virtual teams gather everyone together and spend some time in face-to-face meetings to work through these issues; direct contact is the most effective way for a leader to build relationships, common knowledge, a shared identity, and winning attitudes. Once a common framework has been established, subsequent meetings will not need to be face-to-face; it is important for leaders to assemble all the members together at least once or twice to work through the Rocket Model components.

Lesson 5: Be Deliberate When On-Boarding New Members. We know a person who went through a long hiring process before being selected for a director level position at a large company. During his first two weeks with the company, he never met his new boss, never attended a meeting with his peers, was never told who was on his team, was given a desk in the hallway, and didn't have a phone. He was so frustrated that he joined another company after two weeks. The irony is that he had joined the human resources department of a major telecommunications firm.

Although this story may sound unusual, many leaders believe their responsibility is to recruit new members, and it is the member's responsibility to mesh with their teams. Leaders can use the Rocket Model to accelerate the on-boarding process. Leaders who take an hour or two to review their vision and the team's internal and external constituencies, scorecard, roles and responsibilities matrix, norms, resources, and results to date with the new employee will find this to be time well spent. New recruits often make mistakes because they lack knowledge about team issues and norms; therefore, if leaders can on-board new recruits, rather than leaving them to work things out for themselves, the team will become more productive and cohesive.

Lesson 6: Avoid Common Team-Building Mistakes. The five previous lessons describe some of the more common team-building mistakes: inadequate preparation and planning, failing to set aside enough time to work through team issues, not persisting with team-building efforts, setting up team-building sessions at inopportune times, failing to deal with global and virtual team issues, and abandoning new members. Other common mistakes include operating *groups* as *teams*; failing to clarify the first team; not having a robust framework (such as the Rocket Model) for building and maintaining team and group performance; not identifying key internal and external constituencies; setting vague goals; failing to clarify members' roles or address team killers; wasting time by running poor meetings; playing favorites; failing to articulate a clear and compelling team vision; squandering resources; failing to effectively manage conflict and agreement; and failing to teach teams how to win. Leaders can mismanage in a myriad of ways; however, there are remedies for all these common team-building mistakes. Leaders who truly want to achieve better results through others can meet this goal by understanding and applying the lessons contained in this book.

Conclusion

This chapter describes how the Rocket Model can be used to improve the performance of new and existing teams. Those in charge of new teams should begin by holding an off-site meeting to share their vision and have their teams start working though exercises for each Rocket Model component. The ideal sequence for new teams is to start with Context and then work through Mission, Talent, Norms, Buy-In, Power, Morale, and Results. In many cases it will take several off-sites to work through all of these components, but most leaders will find that this is time well spent and will soon see an increase in team performance.

Leaders in charge of existing teams can use the TAS II and team interviews to determine which components of the Rocket Model need the most improvement. Leaders should first evaluate Context and then assess the functioning of the other components. Leaders should start working on the next component only if the team is scoring well on the preceding components. For example, Mission and Talent should be addressed before Norms and Buy-In, and Norms and Buy-In must be addressed before Power and Morale, etc. Leaders of existing teams usually need to work on Context, Mission, and Talent even if they are not the lowest scoring components because even average scores here can negatively impact team functioning and performance.

We close on the point with which we opened this chapter: building high-performing teams and groups is both a science and an art. The science of building high-performing teams comes from the Rocket Model and its exercises. However, knowing the Rocket Model is no guarantee that leaders will build high-performing teams. They also need to know how to *apply* the Rocket Model components, exercises, and lessons, and this discernment involves some artistic ability—i.e., knowing which exercises to use, when to use them, and how to facilitate team discussions. It usually takes some time to develop the expertise needed to diagnose team functioning accurately and intervene appropriately. There is no magic to building high-performing teams and groups. It just takes leaders who know what to do to improve team performance and achieve better results through others.

New Team Off-Site Goals, Roles, and Agendas

Off-Site I: ACO Leadership Team

Prework:

- Goals, roles, and agenda for the Off-Site I.

- Information packets on customers, competitors, channel partners, industry trends, and financials.

- Building High-Performing Teams article by Gordy Curphy and RT Hogan[89]

- The Theory of the Business article by Peter Drucker[90]

Goals:

- Understand William's vision for the ACO.

- Understand how the Rocket Model can be used to build-high performing teams.

- Understand the context surrounding the ACO.

- Create an ACO scorecard for 2013.

- Clarify roles and responsibilities of the leadership team members.

- Create an operating rhythm for the ACO.

- Enhance commitment to team goals and member roles.
- Create action plans for the next off-site.

Roles:

- William—team leader/facilitator.
- Sue, George, Kemal, Jang, Prasad, Henri, Dianne, and Joan—participants.

Process/Agenda:

Day One

8:00-8:30	Introduction
8:30-9:00	Introduction to High-Performing Teams: The Rocket Model
9:00-9:15	Break
9:15-11:30	Context: Key Constituencies and Assumptions
11:30-12:15	Lunch
12:15-3:00	Mission: Team Scorecards
3:00-3:15	Break
3:15-4:30	Talent: Roles and Responsibility Matrix
4:30-6:00	Buy-in: Journey Lines
6:00-	Social and Dinner

Day Two

8:00-8:30	Review and Reflection
8:30-10:00	Mission: Team Scorecard Review
10:00-10:15	Break
10:15-12:00	Norms: Operating Rhythm
12:00-12:45	Lunch
12:45-3:30	Team Action Planning and Break
3:30-3:45	Break
3:45-4:30	Key Messages, Next Steps, and Off-Site +s and -s

Off-Site II: ACO Leadership Team

Prework:

- Goals, roles, and agenda for the Off-Site II.
- ACO scorecard and action plan results to date.
- Action plan and results obtained for the hardware project.
- Instructions for completing the Communications Norms Checklist, Accountability Norms Checklist, and Resource Analysis Exercise Form before the off-site.

Goals:

- Review progress on the ACO scorecard.
- Conduct an After Action Review of the hardware project.
- Identify and resolve issues affecting ACO goal progress.
- Set team communication, decision-making, and accountability norms.
- Identify resource requirements for the ACO.
- Enhance commitment to team goals and member roles.
- Create action plans for the next off-site.

Roles:

- William—team leader/facilitator.
- Sue, George, Kemal, Jang, Prasad, Henri, Dianne, and Joan—participants.

Process/Agenda:

8:00-8:15	Introduction and Goal and Agenda Review
8:15-9:45	ACO Scorecard and Action Plan Review
9:45-10:00	Break
10:00-11:30	Hardware Project After Action Review
11:30-12:15	Lunch
12:15-1:00	Norms: Communication
1:00-1:45	Norms: Decision-Making

1:45-2:00	Break
2:00-2:45	Norms: Accountability
2:45-4:00	Power: Resource Requirements
4:00-5:00	Action Planning
5:00-5:30	Key Messages, Next Steps, and Off-Site +s and −s

Off-Site III: ACO Leadership Team

Day One

Prework:

- Goals, roles, and agenda for the Off-Site III-Day One.
- ACO scorecard and action plan results to date.

Goals:

- Review progress on the ACO scorecard and action plans.
- Identify and resolve issues affecting ACO goal progress.
- Enhance commitment to team goals and member roles.
- Prepare for the indirect report team-building session.
- Create action plans for the next off-site.

Roles:

- William—team leader/facilitator.
- Sue, George, Kemal, Jang, Prasad, Henri, Dianne, and Joan—participants.

Process/Agenda:

8:00-8:15	Introduction and Goal and Agenda Review
8:15-9:45	ACO Scorecard and Action Plan Review
9:45-10:00	Break
10:00-11:30	Barrier Identification and Productive Dialogues

11:30-12:15	Lunch
12:15-2:15	Force Field Analysis and Action Planning for Top Three Barriers
2:15-2:30	Break
2:30-5:00	Preparation for Day Two Session
5:00-5:30	Key Messages, Next Steps, and Off-Site +s and −s

ACO Leadership Team and Indirect Reports

Day Two

Prework:

- Goals, roles, and agenda for the Off-Site III-Day Two.

- Key internal and external constituencies and assumptions; ACO scorecard and progress to date; roles and responsibility matrix for ACO leadership team; leadership team norms; and ACO resource requirements.

- Building High-Performing Teams article by Gordy Curphy and RT Hogan[91]

Goals:

- Understand William's vision for the ACO.

- Understand how the Rocket Model can be used to build high-performing teams.

- Understand the context surrounding the ACO.

- Understand the ACO scorecard for 2013.

- Understand the roles and responsibilities of the leadership team members.

- Understand the operating rhythm and communication, decision-making, and accountability norms for the ACO.

- Understand the resource requirements for the ACO.

- Apply the Rocket Model to their respective staff teams.

- Create action plans for creating high performing staff teams.

Roles:

- William--team leader/facilitator.
- Sue, George, Kemal, Jang, Prasad, Henri, Dianne, and Joan—facilitators.
- Indirect reports—participants.

Process/Agenda:

8:00-8:30	Introduction
8:30-9:00	Introduction to High Performing Teams: The Rocket Model
9:00-10:00	Context: Internal and External Constituency Review (Joan)
10:00-10:15	Break
10:15-11:15	Mission: ACO Scorecard Review (Dianne)
11:15-11:30	Leadership Team Roles and Responsibilities Review (Prasad)
11:30-12:00	Norms Review (Kemal)
12:00-12:45	Lunch
12:45-1:30	Resources Review (Sue)
1:30-4:30	Applying The Rocket Model to Staff Teams (Break Outs)

- Identify staff team constituencies
- Create staff team scorecards
- Create staff roles and responsibility matrices
- Set staff team operating rhythm and norms
- Create staff team action plans

4:30-5:30	Staff Team Report Outs
5:30-6:00	Key Messages, Next Steps, and Off-Site +s and -s

Off-Site IV: ACO Leadership Team

Prework:

- Goals, roles, and agenda for the Off-Site IV.
- Instructions for completing TAS II.
- ACO scorecard and action plan results to date.

Goals:

- Review progress on the ACO scorecard and action plans.
- Review TAS II results.
- Identify and resolve issues affecting ACO goal progress.
- Enhance commitment to team goals and member roles.
- Prepare for the indirect report team building session.
- Create action plans for the next off-site.

Roles:

- William—team leader/facilitator.
- Sue, George, Kemal, Jang, Prasad, Henri, Dianne, and Joan—participants.

Process/Agenda:

8:00-8:15	Introduction and Goal and Agenda Review
8:15-9:45	ACO Scorecard and Action Plan Review
9:45-10:00	Break
10:00-11:30	TAS II Results Review
11:30-12:15	Lunch
12:15-1:15	Roles and Responsibilities Discussion and Update
2:15-2:30	Break
2:30-3:30	Operating Rhythm Discussion and Update
3:30-5:00	Force Field Analyses and Action Planning
5:00-5:30	Key Messages, Next Steps, and Off-Site +s and −s

End Notes

Chapter 1

[1] J. Druett, *Island of the Lost: Shipwrecked on the End of the World* (Chapel Hills, NC: Algonquin Books of Chapel Hill, 2005).

[2] A. Lansing, *Endurance: Shackleton's Incredible Voyage* (New York: Carroll & Graf Publishers, 1999).

[3] B. Tuchman, *Stilwell and the American Experience in China, 1911-45.* (New York: The Macmillan Company, 1971).

[4] R. Hogan, *Personality and the Fate of Organizations* (Mahwah, NJ: Lawrence Erlbaum & Associates, 2007).

[5] J. R. Hackman, "Why Teams Don't Work: An Interview with J. Richard Hackman," *Harvard Business Review* (May 2009). Reprint R0905H.

[6] R. Hogan.

[7] P. Lencioni, *The Five Dysfunctions of a Team: A Leadership Fable* (San Francisco: Jossey-Bass, 2002).

[8] Hackman, "Why Teams Don't Work: An Interview with J. Richard Hackman."

Chapter 2

[9] B. Tuckman, "The Developmental Sequence in Small Groups,"' *Psychological Bulletin* 63 (1965): 384–399.

[10] J. R. Hackman, *Groups That Work (and Those That Don't)* (San Francisco: Jossey-Bass, 1990).

[11] R. Ginnett, "Team Effectiveness Leadership Model: Design & Diagnosis," (presented at 12th Annual International Conference on Work Teams, Dallas, Texas, 2001).

[12] Lencioni.

[13] G. Curphy and R. Hogan, "A Guide to Building High-Performing Teams," unpublished manuscript, 2010.

[14] Tuckman.

[15] R. Hughes, R. Ginnett, and G. Curphy, *Leadership: Enhancing the Lessons of Experience (7th ed.)* (Burr Ridge, IL: McGraw-Hill Irwin, 2011).

[16] Hackman, *Groups That Work (and Those That Don't)*.

[17] Ibid.

[18] Ginnett, "Team Effectiveness Leadership Model: Design & Diagnosis."

[19] R. Ginnett, "Crews as Groups: Their Formation and Their Leadership"' in *Crew Resource Management*, ed. B. Kanki, R. Helmreich, and J. Anca (San Diego, CA: Academic Press, 2010).

[20] Hughes, Ginnett, and Curphy.

[21] Lencioni.

[22] J. Katzenbach and B. Smith, *The Wisdom of Teams* (Boston: HarperBusiness, 1994).

[23] P. Myers and K. Myers, *The Myers-Briggs Type Indicator Step II (Form Q) Profile* (Palo Alto, CA: Consulting Psychologists Press, 2003).

[24] Curphy and Hogan.

[25] R. Hogan.

[26] Hackman, "Why Teams Don't Work: An Interview with J. Richard Hackman."

[27] G. Curphy, *The Team Assessment Survey II* (Eagan, MN: Advantis Research and Consulting, 2011).

Chapter 3

[28] W. H. McNeill, *The Pursuit of Power: Technology, Armed Force, and Society since A.D. 1000 (Chicago, IL: The University of Chicago Press, 1984)*.

[29] R. Charan, S. Drotter, and J. Noel, *The Leadership Pipeline: How to Build a Leadership-Powered Company* (San Francisco, CA: Jossey Bass, 2001).

[30] P. Drucker, "The Theory of the Business," *Harvard Business Review*, September-October, 1994, Reprint 94506.

Chapter 4

[31] P. Drucker, *The Executive in Action* (New York: HarperCollins Publishing, 1996).

[32] S. Kerr, "On the Folly of Rewarding A, While Hoping for B," *Academy of Management Executive* 9, no. 1 (1995): 7–14.

[33] R. Kaplan and D. Norton, *The Balanced Scorecard: Translating Strategy into Action* (Boston, MA: Harvard Business School Press, 1996).

[34] E. Locke and G. Latham, "Building a Practically Useful Theory of Goal Setting and Task Motivation: A 35-Year Odyssey," *American Psychologist* 57, no. 9 (2002): 705–18.

[35] Hughes, Ginnett, and Curphy.

[36] E. Locke, "Goal Setting Theory and Its Applications to the World of Business," *Academy of Management Executive* 18, no. 4 (2004): 124–125.

[37] G. Latham, "The Motivational Benefits of Goal Setting," *Academy of Management Executive* 18, no. 4 (2004): 126–129.

Chapter 5

[38] J. Collins, *Good to Great.* (New York, NY: HarperCollins Publishing, 2001).

[39] E. Larrabee, *Commander in Chief: Franklin Delano Roosevelt, His Lieutenants, and Their War*. (Annapolis, MD: Naval Institute Press, 2004).

[40] Drucker, *The Executive in Action*.

[41] Hackman, "Why Teams Don't Work: An Interview with J. Richard Hackman."

[42] Hackman, *Groups That Work (and Those That Don't).*

[43] Hughes, Ginnett, and Curphy.

[44] Ibid.

[45] Hackman, *Groups That Work (and Those That Don't).*

[46] G. Curphy and M. Roellig, *Followership* (North Oaks, MN: Curphy Consulting Corporation, 2010).

[47] Hughes, Ginnett, and Curphy.

[48] Curphy and Roellig.

[49] Hughes, Ginnett, and Curphy.

[50] Curphy and Roellig.

[51] T. Casciaro and M. Sousa Lobo, "Competent Jerks, Lovable Fools, and the Formation of Social Networks," (June 2005), Reprint R0506E.

Chapter 6

[52] Hackman, "Why Teams Don't Work: An Interview with J. Richard Hackman."

[53] Curphy and Hogan.

[54] Hughes, Ginnett, and Curphy.

[55] Lencioni.

[56] Hackman, "Why Teams Don't Work: An Interview with J. Richard Hackman."

[57] R. Dallek, *Lyndon B. Johnson*: *Portrait of a President* (New York: Oxford University Press, 2004).

[58] J. Harvey, *The Abilene Paradox and Other Mediations on Management* (San Francisco: Jossey-Bass, 1988).

[59] G. Orwell, . (New York: Harcourt Brace & Company, 1946).

Chapter 7

[60] J. Kouzes and B. Posner, *The Credibility Factor* (San Francisco: Jossey-Bass, 1996).

[61] Personnel Decisions International, *PROFILOR® Certification Manual*. Minneapolis, MN: Author, 2001.

[62] Hughes, Ginnett, and Curphy.

[63] J. Strange and M. Mumford, "The Origins of Vision: Charismatic versus Ideological Leadership," *Leadership Quarterly* 13, no.4 (2002): 343–378.

[64] J. Mio, R. Riggio, S. Levin, and R. Reese, "Presidential Leadership and Charisma: The Effects of Metaphor," *Leadership Quarterly* 15, no.3 (2005): 287–294.

[65] L. Naidoo and R. Lord, "Speech Imagery and Perceptions of Charisma: The Mediating Role of Positive Affect," *Leadership Quarterly* 19, no.3 (2008): 283–296.

[66] Hughes, Ginnett, and Curphy.

[67] J. Stockdale, *A Vietnam Experience: Ten Tears of Reflection* (Stanford, CA: Hoover Institute, Stanford University, 1984).

[68] Hughes, Ginnett, and Curphy.

[69] J. Bono and R. Ilies, "Charisma, Positive Emotion, and Mood Contagion," *Leadership Quarterly* 17, no. 3 (2006): 317—334.

[70] Hughes, Ginnett, and Curphy.

Chapter 8

[71] T. Kean, L. Hamilton, R. Ben-Veniste, B. Kerrey, F. Fielding, J. Lehman, J. Gorelick, T. Roemer, S. Gorton, and J. Thompson, *The 9/11 Commission Report* (New York: W.W. Norton & Company, 2004).

[72] The National Commission on Fiscal Responsibility and Reform, *The Moment of Truth* (Washington, D.C.: The White House, December 2010). http://www.fiscal commission. gov/ sites/ fiscalcommission.gov/files/documents/TheMomentof Truth12_1_2010.pdf (accessed on March 22, 2012).

[73] Ibid.

[74] J. Fabian, "Rand Paul: Fiscal Commission Report Doesn't Go Far Enough," *The Hill* (November 12, 2010).

[75] Hackman, "Why Teams Don't Work: An Interview with J. Richard Hackman."

[76] R. Lardner, "Afghanistan's Rebuilding Looms As Sequel To Iraq's," http://www. huffingtonpost.com/2009/05/24/afghanistans-rebuilding-l_n_207201.html (accessed on March 22, 2012)

Chapter 9

[77] Curphy and Hogan.

[78] Hughes, Ginnett, and Curphy.

[79] D. Dotlich and P. Cairo, *Why CEOs Fail: The 11 Behaviors That Can Derail Your Climb to the Top and How to Manage Them* (New York: Wiley, 2001).

[80] J. Hogan, R. Hogan, and R. Kaiser, "Managerial Derailment" in *APA Handbook of Industrial and Organizational Psychology*, Vol. 3. ed. S. Zedeck. (Washington, DC: American Psychological Association, 2001) 555-576.

[81] I. Janus, *Groupthink (2nd ed.)* (Boston: Houghton Mifflin, 1982).

[82] Hughes, Ginnett, and Curphy.

[83] Harvey.

84 Hughes, Ginnett, and Curphy.

85 Curphy.

86 Lencioni.

Chapter 10

87 R. Knowling, *You Can Get There From Here: My Journey From Struggle to Success* (New York: Portfolio/Penguin, 2011).

88 K. Lewin, "Field Theory and Experiment in Social Psychology: Concepts and Methods," 44 (1939): 868—896.

Chapter 11

89 Curphy and Hogan.

90 P. Drucker, "The Theory of the Business."

91 Curphy and Hogan.

References

Bono, J. and R. Ilies. "Charisma, Positive Emotion, and Mood Contagion." *Leadership Quarterly* 17, no. 3 (2006): 317–334 .

Casciaro, T. and M. Sousa Lobo. "Competent Jerks, Lovable Fools, and the Formation of Social Networks." *Harvard Business Review* (June 2005). Reprint R0506E.

Charan, R., S. Drotter, and J. Noel. *The Leadership Pipeline: How to Build a Leadership-Powered Company.* San Francisco: Jossey Bass, 2001.

Collins, J. *Good to Great.* New York: HarperCollins Publishing, 2001.

Curphy, G. *The Team Assessment Survey II.* Eagan, MN: Advantis Research and Consulting, 2011.

Curphy, G. and R. Hogan. "A Guide to Building High-Performing Teams." unpublished manuscript, 2010.

Curphy, G. and M. Roellig. *Followership.* North Oaks, MN: Curphy Consulting Corporation, 2010

Dallek, R. *Lyndon B. Johnson: Portrait of a President*. New York: Oxford University Press, 2004.

Dotlich, D. and P. Cairo. *Why CEOs Fail: The 11 Behaviors That Can Derail Your Climb to the Top and How to Manage Them*. New York: Wiley, 2001.

Drucker, P. *The Executive in Action.* New York: HarperCollins Publishing,1996.

Drucker, P. "The Theory of the Business." *Harvard Business Review* (September-October, 1994). Reprint 94506.

Druett, J. *Island of the Lost: Shipwrecked on the End of the World.* Chapel Hills, NC: Algonquin Books of Chapel Hill, 2005.

Fabian, J. "Rand Paul: Fiscal Commission Report Doesn't Go Far Enough." *The Hill* (November 12, 2010).

Ginnett, R. "Crews as Groups: Their Formation and Their Leadership"' in *Crew Resource Management*. Edited by B. Kanki, R. Helmreich, and J. Anca. San Diego, CA: Academic Press, 2010.

Ginnett, R. "Team Effectiveness Leadership Model: Design & Diagnosis." Presented at 12th Annual International Conference on Work Teams, Dallas, Texas, 2001.

Hackman, J.R. *Groups That Work (and Those That Don't)*. San Francisco: Jossey-Bass, 1990.

Hackman, J.R. "Why Teams Don't Work: An Interview with J. Richard Hackman." *Harvard Business Review* (May 2009). Reprint R0905H.

Harvey, J. *The Abilene Paradox and Other Mediations on Management*. San Francisco: Jossey-Bass, 1988.

Hogan, J., R. Hogan, and R. Kaiser. "Managerial Derailment." *APA Handbook of Industrial and Organizational Psychology*, Vol. 3. Edited by S. Zedeck. Washington, D.C.: American Psychological Association (2001): 555—576.

Hogan, R. *Personality and the Fate of Organizations.* Mahwah, NJ: Lawrence Erlbaum & Associates, 2007.

Hughes, R., R. Ginnett, and G. Curphy. *Leadership: Enhancing the Lessons of Experience (7th ed.).* Burr Ridge, IL: McGraw-Hill Irwin, 2011.

Janus, I. *Groupthink (2nd ed.).* Boston: Houghton Mifflin, 1982.

Kaplan, R. and D. Norton. *The Balanced Scorecard: Translating Strategy into Action.* Boston, MA: Harvard Business School Press, 1996.

Katzenbach, K. and B. Smith, *The Wisdom of Teams.* Boston: HarperBusiness, 1994.

Kean, T., L. Hamilton, R. Ben-Veniste, B. Kerrey, F. Fielding, J. Lehman, J. Gorelick, T. Roemer, S. Gorton, and J. Thompson. *The 9/11 Commission Report*. New York: W.W. Norton & Company, 2004.

Kerr, S. "On the Folly of Rewarding A, While Hoping for B." *Academy of Management Executive 9*, no. 1 (1995): 7—14.

Knowling, R. *You Can Get There From Here: My Journey From Struggle to Success.* New York: Portfolio/Penguin, 2011.

Kouzes, J. and B. Posner. *The Credibility Factor*. San Francisco: Jossey-Bass, 1996.

Lansing, S. *Endurance: Shackleton's Incredible Voyage.* New York: Carroll & Graf Publishers, 1999.

Lardner, R. "Afghanistan's Rebuilding Looms As Sequel To Iraq's," *Huffington Post.* http://www.huffingtonpost.com/2009/05/24/afghanistans-rebuilding-l_n_207201.html (accessed March 22, 2012).

Larrabee, E. *Commander in Chief: Franklin Delano Roosevelt, His Lieutenants, and Their War.* Annapolis, MD: Naval Institute Press, 2004.

Latham, G. "The Motivational Benefits of Goal Setting." *Academy of Management Executive 18*, no. 4 (2004): 126–129.

Lencioni, P. *The Five Dysfunctions of a Team: A Leadership Fable.* San Francisco: Jossey-Bass, 2002.

Lewin, K. "Field Theory and Experiment in Social Psychology: Concepts and Methods." *American Journal of Sociology 44* (1939): 868–896.

Locke, E. "Goal Setting Theory and Its Applications to the World of Business." *Academy of Management Executive 18*, no. 4. (2004): 124–125.

Locke, E. and G. Latham. "Building a Practically Useful Theory of Goal Setting and Task Motivation: A 35-Year Odyssey." *American Psychologist 57*, no. 9. (2002): 705–18.

McNeill, W.H. *The Pursuit of Power: Technology, Armed Force, and Society since A.D. 1000.* Chicago: The University of Chicago Press, 1984.

Mio, J., R. Riggio, S. Levin, and R. Reese. "Presidential Leadership and Charisma: The Effects of Metaphor." *Leadership Quarterly 15*, no. 3 (2005): 287–294.

Myers, P. and K. Myers. *The Myers-Briggs Type Indicator Step II (Form Q) Profile.* Palo Alto, CA: Consulting Psychologists Press, 2003.

Naidoo, L. and R. Lord. "Speech Imagery and Perceptions of Charisma: The Mediating Role of Positive Affect." *Leadership Quarterly 19*, no. 3 (2008): 283–296.

The National Commission on Fiscal Responsibility and Reform, *The Moment of Truth.* Washington, D.C.: The White House, December 2010. http://www.fiscal commission. gov/ sites/ fiscalcommission.gov/files/documents/TheMomentof Truth12_1_2010.pdf (accessed on March 22, 2012)

Orwell, G. *Animal Farm.* New York: Harcourt Brace & Company, 1946.

Personnel Decisions International. *PROFILOR® Certification Manual.* Minneapolis, MN: Author, 2001.

Stockdale, J. *A Vietnam Experience: Ten Tears of Reflection*. Stanford, CA: Hoover Institute, Stanford University, 1984.

Strange, J. and M. Mumford. "The Origins of Vision: Charismatic versus Ideological Leadership." *Leadership Quarterly 13*, no. 4 (2002): 343–378.

Tuchman, B. *Stilwell and the American Experience in China, 1911-45.* New York: The Macmillan Company, 1971.

Tuckman, B. "The Developmental Sequence in Small Groups."' *Psychological Bulletin 63* (1965): 384–399.